Real Cash

Real Cash

by ROBERT DOMICO

ReadersMagnet, LLC

Real Cash
Copyright © 2019 by Robert Domico

Published in the United States of America
ISBN Paperback: 978-1-948864-74-9
ISBN Hardback: 978-1-948864-75-6
ISBN eBook: 978-1-948864-76-3

All rights reserved. No part of this publication may be reproduced, stored in a retrieval system or transmitted in any way by any means, electronic, mechanical, photocopy, recording or otherwise without the prior permission of the author except as provided by USA copyright law.

The opinions expressed by the author are not necessarily those of ReadersMagnet, LLC.

ReadersMagnet, LLC
10620 Treena Street, Suite 230 | San Diego, California, 92131 USA
1.619.354.2643 | www.readersmagnet.com

Book design copyright © 2019 by ReadersMagnet, LLC. All rights reserved.
Cover design by Ericka Obando
Interior design by Manolito Bastasa

Contents

Preface 11
Introduction 13

Chapter 1	Purchasing an Existing Shopping Center............	35
Chapter 2	How to Syndicate a Large Restaurant.................	37
Chapter 3	Putting a Shopping Center Deal Together from Scratch..	39
Chapter 4	Starting Your Own Business Brokerage...............	41
Chapter 5	Highest and Best Use..	43
Chapter 6	How to Purchase a Large Shopping Center.........	45
Chapter 7	Once You Acquire a Large Restaurant	47
Chapter 8	Developing a Rural Area Piece of Land	50
Chapter 9	How to Own Many Condos, Collecting Rent without Paying Any Mortgage Payments	52
Chapter 10	Developing Raw Land and Making It Very Valuable..	54
Chapter 11	Proven System to Purchase Houses and Have Your Tenants Pay Off the Mortgages for You......	56
Chapter 12	Hot to Put a Casino Deal Together......................	58
Chapter 13	How to Pull Money out of Real Estate, with No Money...	64
Chapter 14	How to Own 51 Percent of a Law Firm and Create a Million-Dollar Equity in a House..........	66

Chapter 15	How to Flip Large Properties without Actually Purchasing Them 68
Chapter 16	How to Syndicate 71
Chapter 17	The 1031 Exchange 73
Chapter 18	How to Set Up a Web Page to Advertise Your Syndication Business 77
Chapter 19	How to Take Useless Land and Make It Very Valuable 79
Chapter 20	More Development of Useless Empty Land 81
Chapter 21	How to Develop an Over-Fifty-Five Community 83
Chapter 22	How to Put Together a Trailer Park 86
Chapter 23	Building a Marina with Very Little Waterfront: The New Wave 88
Chapter 24	How to Build a Floating Home Park 90
Chapter 25	How to Develop a Horse Stall Condominium Complex 92
Chapter 26	How to Develop a Condo Hotel in a Resort Area 94
Chapter 27	How to Syndicate a Feedlot 96
Chapter 28	How to Syndicate a Foreign 98
Chapter 29	How to Syndicate an Apartment Building and Make It into Condos or Co-Ops 100
Chapter 30	How to Syndicate a Condominium Shopping Center 102
Chapter 31	How to Convert an Office Building into Condo Offices 104
Chapter 32	How to Convert a Warehouse into Condominiums 106
Chapter 33	How to Convert a Warehouse into a Ministorage Facility 110
Chapter 34	How to Convince Lawyers, Accountants, Engineers, and Architects They Should Work for You on a Contingency Basis 112

Chapter 35	How to Put Together a Fleet of Charter Boats for Lease or to Syndicate and Sell Them Out to Fifty Owners Per Boat One Per Week Each Ownership to Time-Share	114
Chapter 36	Owning Land under Very Valuable Property Is Definitely a Way to Create Great Wealth	116
Chapter 37	Monologue of a Salesman	120
Chapter 38	How to Syndicate Condominium Boat Slips	122
Chapter 39	How to Get Very Wealthy on Residential Real Estate Starting with Your Residence	125
Chapter 40	How to Use Your Commissions from Your Business Brokerage or Real Estate Company to Make Bigger and Better Deals	127
Chapter 41	My First Syndication: Lucien's Old Tavern	129
Chapter 42	Schrul's Restaurant: My Second Syndication	134
Chapter 43	My Third Syndication: Executive Banquets	137
Chapter 44	How to Put Syndication Together with Mirrors	139
Chapter 45	How to Foreclose on Properties	141
Chapter 46	How to Purchase Business Cheap, Build Them Up, and Sell Them	144
Chapter 47	Taking Over Large Business from the Bank That Are in Bankruptcy	146
Chapter 48	Foreclosing on Properties Using Adverse Possession	148
Chapter 49	Going into Business for Yourself	151
Chapter 50	How to Syndicate an Energy Windmill Company to Supply Electricity to Small Cities	154
Chapter 51	How to Form a Real Estate Company with Syndication	158
Chapter 52	How to Put a Factory Syndication Together	160
Chapter 53	How to Be a Comedian, Make Friends and Audiences Laugh	162
Chapter 54	How People Get Real Estate through Commercial or Civil Conspiracy	165

Chapter 55	The Master of Mirrors 168
Chapter 56	How to Get Real Estate by Heir Hunting, Deed Raiding, and Redemption without Cause 170
Chapter 57	How to Make One Million Cash Tax Free on One Deal by Buying Real Estate 173
Chapter 58	How to Syndicate New Jersey Tax Sale Certificates and Gain up to 25 Percent Interest in Properties with No Money 175
Chapter 59	You're Better Off with No State Licenses If You're Doing My Deals 177
Chapter 60	Foreclosure 179
Chapter 61	Mortgage Cash Flow Notes, Another Business for the Coming Bad Times 181

Chapter 1	Putting Together a Rooming House 185
Chapter 2	Converting Residential Zoning into Professional Zoning or Highest and Best Use 187
Chapter 3	Putting Together a Shopping Center from Scratch Is Easier Than You Think 190
Chapter 4	Putting Together a Self-Storage Complex from an Existing Warehouse or Building from Scratch 192
Chapter 5	Buying Condominiums to Rent Out with a Good Yield of Income versus Expenses 194
Chapter 6	Building a Condominium Slip Marina Changing the Existing Marina into Highest and Best Use 197
Chapter 7	Buying a Shopping Center and Converting It to Condominium Stores to Make a Lot of Money 200
Chapter 8	How to Control Millions of Dollars' Worth of Real Estate without Actually Purchasing It 203
Chapter 9	The Master of Mirrors 208
Chapter 10	Putting a Billboard Company Together from Scratch and Making Money off the Rest of the Land 212

Chapter 11	Buying Something and Making It Worth Much More by Doing Several Things to It 214
Chapter 12	Building a Trailer Park Is Relatively Easy If You Have the Zoning 218
Chapter 13	Building a Water Home Park, Selling the Homes, Renting the Homes, Selling Out the Spaces, Renting Out the Spaces, or All of the Above 220
Chapter 14	Purchasing Land, Getting It Approved, and Selling It to a Developer 223
Chapter 15	Pulling Money out of Real Estate by Refinancing 225
Chapter 16	The Master of Mirrors Is the Master of Syndications 227
Chapter 17	Syndicating a Co-Op Situation for a Large Profit 231
Chapter 18	Make Money in Real Estate by Opening a Business Brokerage 233
Chapter 19	Making Money on Time-Share 236
Chapter 20	Finding Land and Making It Valuable 238
Chapter 21	Opening a Large Restaurant with Banquet Facilities 241
Chapter 22	Building a Factory Is a Windfall 244
Chapter 23	How to Put Together an Energy Company 246
Chapter 24	Going into Business for Your Self 248
Chapter 25	Dealing with the Bankruptcy Court to Purchase Real Estate and Business 251
Chapter 26	Adverse Possession Is a Way to Foreclose on Properties 254
Chapter 27	Purchase Business Cheap and Sell Them for a Profit 257
Chapter 28	Foreclosing on Properties 259
Chapter 29	Put a Syndication Together and Own the Property 100 Percent Yourself in Five Years 262
Chapter 30	Putting Your Commission Back into Deals to Put up Your Part of the Money 265

Chapter 31	How to Get Very Wealthy on Residential Real Estate Starting with Your Own Residence	268
Chapter 32	Buying a Marina and Converting It to Condominium Slips	270
Chapter 33	The Salesman	272
Chapter 34	Land under Valuable Property	274
Chapter 35	Time-Share a Large Boat for Obscene Profits	277
Chapter 36	Warehouse to Mini Storage Conversion: Six Dollars a Foot Income to Twenty-Five Dollars a Foot Income.	279
Chapter 37	Converting a Warehouse into a Condominium Warehouse	281
Chapter 38	Converting an Office Building into Condo Offices	284
Chapter 39	Making an Apartment Building into Condos or Co-Ops	286
Chapter 40	Resort Area Condo Conversion and Hotel Condos	288
Chapter 41	Building an Over-Fifty-Five Community	290
Chapter 42	Develop Empty Land	292
Chapter 43	How to Do a 1031 Exchange	294
Chapter 44	Beware of Real Estate Fraud: IRS Is Watching	298
Chapter 45	Import-Export Business	302
Chapter 46	Mortgage Cash Flow Notes	303
Chapter 47	Starting a Home Loan Modification Company	305
Chapter 48	Heir Hunting, Deed Raiding, and Redemption without Cause	307
Chapter 49	Getting Rich on Tax Sale Certificates	309
Chapter 50	Large Development Twenty Million Dollar Build Out	311
Chapter 51	Making Large Parcels of Land into Millions of Dollars	314
Chapter 52	The Great Approval Process	316

Preface

Did you ever wake up one morning and say, "I'm going to make a million dollars in one year, and I'm not going to use a dime of my money to do so?"

My book Forty Years in the Real Estate Business: How to Make One Million Dollars a Year in Real Estate with No Money is designed so that the reader can put together multimillion-dollar deals with literally no money.

There have been a lot of books written about real estate, but they mostly deal with residential houses and not the big deals that make the most money.

Every deal is almost exactly the same; the only difference is the size. Larger deals are actually easier to put together than smaller deals. A large deal has attorneys on both sides of the transaction; they either have the financing or they don't.

There really is nothing you have to do other than introduce the parties. My book is designed to make it very easy for the reader to put many large deals together with little or no effort.

I will attempt to give you, the reader, the knowledge to put together large deals, form large and small syndications, and wind up owning the properties free and clear, with you as the 100 percent owner.

The reader will understand financing, how to get around with it, and how to do creative financing where needed, how to turn a simple piece of land or a building into a multimillion-dollar complex, and how to use other people's money to your best advantage.

Introduction

---❁---

My father came to this country with his mother from Italy. After arriving at Ellis Island, they moved to South Jersey. After his mother raised him, he became a glassblower and then he went into the war as an infantry soldier.

My mother, the daughter of a junk dealer, was born in South Jersey. Most of my mother's family went to South America to build the city of Rio de Janeiro from the old country before her father came to this country.

On the night she was born, her father went to some of his friends to play cards. In those days, they played a game called "patron and patron," wherein a suit means "boss and second boss." The idea is to win the hand and get a drink.

So my grandfather was feeling pretty good by the time he left his friend's house. When he was walking home, he passed a railroad crossing where a couple of years before, a man and a horse were crossing the tracks and a train came and ran them over.

My grandfather thought he saw the ghost of the man and horse, so he started to run home. When he got there, my mother had already been born; the midwife was still there when he walked in. My grandmother was very angry with him for not being there when my mother was born, but she forgave him because he was so scared from the ghosts that he saw.

My father was looking for bicycle parts one day and walked in to my grandfather's junkyard and met my mother. My parents got married and moved into a house, which became a duplex on five acres in Landisville, New Jersey. My father had a laundry company where he would pick up the dirty laundry, take it to a cleaning plant, and return it to the customers.

We lived about thirty miles from Philadelphia and every Sunday, people would come to visit my family—many people from the city.

Mom would bake bread in the big hearth out in the summer kitchen and Pop would break out the wine that he made. Life was wonderful.

Before I was born, Pop came home one day and there was a big fire across the street. This small town that my family lived in didn't have a fire company. Dad jumped in his car and drove to the next big town and got the fire company to come. By the time he got back, the six houses across the street that were joined together like townhouses were burned to the ground.

So the next day, my father went out and bought a fireman's hat, stood out on the highway, held out the hat, and started collecting for a fire engine for the town. Eventually, he and a couple of neighbors built a firehouse, and they made Pop the fire chief. Pop was the fire chief for years. I remember years later at my father's funeral that the fire company presented Mom with a nice check.

Pop decided to get out of the laundry business and purchase a diner. Mom was against it for she was happy in her present environment. So Pop sold the house and made a major career change, moved about thirty miles away, and purchased a house and a diner a block away.

I was one-year-old when we moved, so I wasn't much of a help, but my brothers and sisters—there were seven of us in all—worked in the diner.

Mom worked in the kitchen, Grand mom peeled potatoes, and Dad worked the front of the house. We had the first diner in the state of New Jersey with spaghetti and meatballs in it. It was twenty cents without meatballs and twenty-five cents with meatballs.

Pop had a diner, like a lot of Italians in the forties; all the diners were owned by Italians. Then the Greeks came over in the fifties and bought most of them out.

My father and I were very close when I was growing up; he taught me many things. He used to say, "Stay in the diner business. It will always treat you well. It's the best business in the world."

The breakfast will come in from 6:00 a.m. to 11:00 a.m. every day, like clockwork; the lunch people will be there after that. Then the first coffee break in the afternoon will be from one to four, and then dinner is always good. After dinner, you have your early-movie people and then the later-movie people after eleven. Then you have your early go-outers, and then the drunks come in about 2:00 a.m., and then the fishermen at 4:30 a.m., and so on twenty-four hours a day—never a dull moment.

A friend told me to never marry a beautiful woman. A beautiful woman will leave you and an ugly woman will leave you too, but so what. He said, "Behind every successful man is a beautiful woman, and behind every beautiful woman is a beautiful behind."

When I was eighteen, I was in the naval reserve, and I decided to go on a "kiddy cruise"—that's an expression for one who goes active navy and gets out one day before he's twenty-one. I went in the navy aboard in the Destroyer Ingraham DD 694. The ship I was on was sunk five times by kamikazes in World War II; it had campaign ribbons all over the side of it.

I walked on the ship and it was a real trip. The ship was decorated for Christmas; it had lights from the bow, to the top of the mast, and then down to the fantail.

We got underway the next day for the Northern Atlantic; it was cold and wet. I remember how the ship bobbed around like a cork amidst the huge waves; the ship was 365 feet long and forty feet wide.

On about the eighth day I was on the ship, I had scullery duty. (I worked in the kitchen or the gallery, as it was called.) I and another sailor were emptying the garbage can off the fantail that night when a huge wave came over and washed us both overboard. The ship did a 360-degree turn and rescued me, but the other guy drowned; they never found his body. I remember feeling guilty about that for a long time after. I had hypothermia for about a week after that, but it was mostly a traumatic experience. The waves were fifty feet high and the water was freezing.

The first port we hit was Ireland, and it was quite unique as I remember. They had this big dance hall with different age groups; the earlier it was, the younger the age. The dances were from 11:00 a.m. to 3:00 p.m., 3:00 a.m. to 6:00 p.m., then 6:00 p.m. to 9:00 p.m., and so on right up until midnight.

The music was mostly American rock and roll. You would meet a girl and then jump into a cab and park near the Queen's Castle. There was no prostitution and the bars were just pubs with old men shooting darts with a pipe in their mouths.

We got underway after about a week there. The next port we hit was Amsterdam, Holland—that was quite different from Ireland. The red light district was called Rim Ran Square. There were store windows up and down this street with a girl sitting in each window. There were truck mirrors on the walls so that the girls could see you coming before you got there, so they could make themselves pretty for you. There was a canal in the middle of the street, and it was appropriately called Canal Street.

There were many neat places that we visited in the Northern Atlantic, the Mediterranean, the Caribbean, and the Red Sea on my long time aboard the ship.

By the time I got out of the service, my brothers had taken over the two diners my father had built, so Pop put me in the deli business.

Pop said, "Come out of the service and I'll put you in the business. I've never worked for anybody in my life, and neither will you. We're born independent, and we'll die that way."

So I opened Bob's Cold Cuts, a deli in Woodbury, New Jersey.

I opened another deli for my wife when I got married, so I had two. I sold both of them, purchased a building, and opened a pizza place with Broasted chicken after that. The marriage didn't last too long; we broke up soon after that.

I sold the pizza place and became director of food service at a local college under independent contract for a couple of years. Then

I opened a coffee shop at an exclusive new apartment complex. After a couple of times of getting it back, I finally sold it. I sold it 4 times, getting it back and keeping the deposits.

After that, my oldest brother, who had taken over the original diner that my father built, died from a heart attack at the age of forty-six. I purchased the place from his wife and doubled the size. I purchased another diner that was closed and moved the two diners together in an L shape, then bricked up the whole front, making it 220 seats. I was twenty-four at that time.

I lost two brothers to heart disease, one at forty-nine and the other at forty-six, and a sister to leukemia at forty-six, but my parents lived until they were eighty-seven and eighty-four.

After operating the diner for a few years, I decided to go to work for someone else for a while. I took a job as executive chef in a large country club in Pennsylvania, where I worked for a while. I got most of my early banquet experience there. I also did some of the high-end parties there, like the wedding of the owner of a large football team, some social affairs of the owner of the several large restaurants, and the wedding to his second wife of the owner of the largest taxi cab company.

We had some of the fanciest affairs imaginable with buffets. Once we had a fruit tree six feet high, starting with a pineapple at the top and making a tree out of fruits. Then we had the chairs covered with fine fabric and the tables covered with fine linens, all color-coordinated weddings—pink bridesmaids' gowns, pink flowers on the table, pink ribbons on the tables, pink lights on the head table, pink icing on the cake. There was also a hindquarter of beef and a hindquarter of veal on the buffet table, unbelievable desserts, and on and on.

Then I got a job as a general manager of food and beverage at a large airport that was seven miles long and three miles wide. The airport was a third the size of an island in Manhattan. The large lounge overlooking the airfield was designed for large affairs. The lounge had marble floors and marble tables. When the planes landed every day at happy hour, there were nineteen waitresses serving cocktails. I learned the catering business big time there when two 747s that couldn't land in New York came down with seven hundred people at 9:00 p.m., after all my crew went home, and I had to feed them.

We had what was called a charter steak, which was ten ounces. I used to put twenty on a baker's pan and stick them in the ovens under the boilers in the confection ovens wherever we could. Airline stewardesses dropped the salads. I stayed there for a few years; it was a large operation with over 125 employees.

While I was there at the airport, I met my second wife. She was from Canada. She had a good job in the school system and then married me and moved down with me where I lived at the time. She got a job in a local business college where I caught her sleeping with the owner of the college. Once again, I got divorced.

After I left the airport, I got a job in a large college in Washington as director of food service. I stayed there for a couple of years, then purchased a restaurant near Washington, and another one down on the Chesapeake Bay, thirty-five miles away.

I purchased the Town Square Inn in Alexandria, Virginia, which was a large nightclub and pizza place. I converted it to a seafood place, much like Chesapeake Bay or a Red Lobster-type operation. I met a beautiful girl there one night, who was Sue Indian and German. We moved in together. She was a great woman. I would come home at 3:00 a.m., and she would ask me if I would like an omelet. She decided to gain a hundred lbs. from 120 lbs. to 220 lbs. So I sent her to a fat farm in Utah, and she lost the hundred lbs., but she never came back.

The place was quite large; it had 220 seats upstairs with restaurant and lounge and three thousand sq. ft. downstairs, which I converted to the largest darting lounge in the Washington area.

I went to WADA, Washington Area Darting Association, where I met and hired two beautiful girls right off the board of directors to teach darts to all my redneck customers. These girls could blow anybody off a dart board, so I wound up with 15, 15-man dart teams, shooting in 15 Washington area pubs every week.

After I was open for a while, one night, a narcotics agent walked in and sold some marijuana to a couple of my customers, and we got busted for being a rendezvous for users of narcotics, and we were closed for forty-five days. I came to find out that my competitor, who I almost ruined when I opened up, had his boat in the same marina as the narcotic agent in Chesapeake, Maryland, thirty-five miles away.

On Monday night, I had singles shooting darts. On Tuesday, I had mixed doubles shooting darts. On Wednesday, I had a cash tournament with all cash returned to players; on Thursday, Friday, and Saturday, I had other types of activities. You could walk in any night with 150 people during my tournaments and hear a pin drop.

Upstairs, I had as many as three hundred for the bands or DJs every night. One time, I had the New Century Platters with the original baritone from the original Platters. I sold tickets out for six nights, two shows a night, 1,800 seats that week for $5 at the door, $9,000 before I sold a drink, and the Platters only got $3,500 for the week.

When I bought the place, it was a country Western club with fifteen to twenty fights out in the parking lot every Saturday night. I promised the chief of police that I would clean the place up. I hired back two of the old bartenders when we opened to tell me who among the patrons ever got in a fight in the place. We flagged them, and within a month, all the fights were history.

One night, I was standing at the front door when two girls came in and said, "We don't want to pay $5 to get in. We just want to say good-bye to the band." They went into the ladies' room. Took off all their clothes, ran around the club twice, and went back into the ladies' room, got dressed, and left.

The restaurant I opened after that was down on the bay. It was originally a casino when Maryland had gambling back in the fifties. What happened was when the new governor was voted in, he decided to knock out the gambling in Maryland, so he closed Marlboro Race Track and closed all the little mom-and-pop casinos in the state.

I bought Ewald's, which was the largest casino there; it was a deserted casino. I purchased it and made a large restaurant and club out of it. It was a huge building with twenty rooms upstairs. I moved some of my dart teams and bands from Alexandria down there and opened up. I didn't know at the time, but North Beach was a Big Bikers Town. The first night I opened up, I sold about 150 dinners. Then the band started to play and these bikers started to walk in.

The bikers said to me, "We won't cause any trouble. If we have any, we will take care of it ourselves."

Well, I ended up having the largest biker's bar in Northern Maryland. For a lot of years, I catered to all their affairs, outings, weddings, you name it.

While I still had the two restaurants that I had opened down south, I was at a marlin tournament in Atlantic City one day. I was always an avid fisherman my whole life. I was in a friend's brand-new boat, and it didn't even have any members on it yet. I remember we were sitting at the bar with the owner at the Atlantic City Marina Restaurant, and he said I built that 850-seat restaurant across the street with expectations of gambling coming to Atlantic City. After he opened it he had a heart attack and closed it; Dom Address 705 Horen Avenue where Golden nugget is now in Atlantic City.

One of my friends—a plumber in Philadelphia, also in the tournament—was sitting across the bar, and he said, "I'd open it if I had somebody to run it."

I jumped in and said, "I'll run it, we'll be partners."

My friend said okay, and we did a five-year lease purchase on the place: $30,000 down and $30,000 a year until we paid off the $600,000 asking price. We put in $30,000 each, agreed, and then bought the restaurant. We opened in May, and we were doing about $30,000 a week.

It was a Red Lobster-type restaurant with seven items that were all-you-can-eat and then a regular seafood menu. In those days, you could put an ad in the paper that says, "If you fit in a size 2 to 7 uniform, you'll get this job." So we hired seventy girls and opened up.

One of the girls I hired, a young twenty-year-old divorcee with beautiful long black hair, caught my eye. We started dating, and she stayed with me for a couple of years after that. She was a horse person who was around horses most of her life. She was an equestrian rider who had many trophies and ribbons for riding in the show ring. Her name was Jo Ann; she was half Jewish and half Cherokee Indian. When I left Atlantic City and went back to Virginia, I took Jo Ann with me.

I gave her a job in my Alexandria restaurant and set her up with a little ranch where we moved a couple of horses in and built a show ring in the front yard. The ranch was five acres with riding trails in the back that went into a state forest—a horse person's dream. One night, when I was out of town, she moved out the horses and her belongings and moved to North [Carolina with some tall lanky cowboy from there. I never saw her again.

The reason I left Atlantic City was because my partner decided to put his wife in the restaurant to help. The first week she was there, she wanted to have all the girls inspected for tuberculosis and venereal disease at about $50 per girl. Then on the second week, she decided to get into a fight with the chef, and he walked out.

So I said to my partner, "Your wife is driving me crazy," and he said, "She's in my eyes."

I said, "You buy me out or I'll buy out."

He said, "I'll buy out," but he never paid me the thirty thousand I put up. I think the whole thing stemmed from the fact that I dated their daughter a couple of times, and then I met Jo Ann, and it was all over.

Where the front door of the restaurant was in Atlantic City was where the front door of Trump Castle is now. What happened after that was gambling came in, and Baron Hilton built a casino for three hundred million dollars. One of the guys in the syndication group was Al Capone's lawyer; the casino board wouldn't issue a gaming license to the group.

Baron Hilton said, "I'll never build a hotel in New Jersey for the rest of my life."

So as the story goes, Donald Trump came along and said to Hilton, "It cost you three hundred million to build it. I'll give you 320 million for it." It became Trump Castle.

There was 473 acres of ground along the Atlantic City Expressway that belonged to a man in California. It started in Pleasantville, going toward Atlantic City, and went almost to the end of the expressway; it was 8,400 feet long.

The property was zoned for eleven non-casino hotels, a five hundred thousand sq. ft. fashion mall, five fast-food suites, and a huge parking lot for six hundred cars. They would move the parking from the center of the expressway and put it on the land; it was a two hundred million-dollar build-out. The DOT was going to build the infrastructure for the one hundred acres of uplands that would be built out. I worked on that deal for the owner for ten years, but it never materialized.

Another deal I tried to put together was a casino in Atlantic City. A friend of mine had a large motel with 250 rooms across the street from this large condominium with three hundred suites. I had an architect design a bridge going from his hotel over to the condo complex. Under the bridge was a view of three other existing casinos in full view.

The man was asking eighteen million for the motel, which had 275 rooms, and the other guy was asking ten million for the condo complex. Instead of spending three hundred million for a casino, you could have put this one together for about seventy-five million, including the casino requirement for five hundred rooms, 25,000 sq. ft. of gambling area and parking.

I flew out to Nevada with the rendering I had made and talked to every mom-and-pop casino operation in the whole state. I was gone over two months but did not get one interested party.

All my friends around me were making a fortune in Atlantic City, buying up all the areas around the existing casinos, blocking any expansion. Another friend of mine actually purchased land before the casinos were built in 1973 and owns land under several casinos and still collects rent today. He also owns many billboards around that town.

After that, I decided to put some syndications together and buy a couple of landmark restaurants and possibly combine the proven performance of these two restaurants for they were both over fifty years old. I would franchise the oldest name: one was Lucien's Old Tavern in Berlin, New Jersey, and the other was Schrul's in McKee City, New Jersey. I set up a banquet business in one of my places that was unbelievable. I had the best chef that I have ever seen in all my years in the business, and I devised a system where the entire restaurant would become a giant banquet facility with no a la carte business at all.

The idea was if I could hit five million a year in that business, the gratuity of 20 percent would net me one million a year before anything else.

I was able to get fifty-four groups to meet there once a month for $10.95, which normally cost $12.95 if you eat there once with a group. I started winter, spring, and fall bridal shows, which I got about twenty-five weddings a year out of.

I began to send out early warning Christmas party letters in September to get the place stimulated. I booked my weddings at 12:00 noon and 5:00 p.m., two a day, in one room to actualize the potential of the place. I wound up doing as many as eight weddings on a Saturday in four rooms, four at twelve and at five to 10:00 p.m. I would wind up doing 2.7 million on my first full year there.

I decided to go back to real estate syndicating, the business that put me on top in the first place. I opened up another commercial industrial real estate agency. One day, I was sitting around with a couple of agents I had hired and in walked Ben Cola.

The young man introduced himself and said, "I lost my $250,000 on options, and now I want to buy real estate. I don't have any money, but I got great credit." Ben and I wound up into partners; our first deal was a 54,000-sq. ft. shopping center.

We put it in agreements with a $5,000 deposit.

I said to the owner, "How much do you want for your center?"

He said, "I want $1.2 million."

I said, "I have to syndicate it, so I am going to need a 20 percent commission because we need 20 percent down to syndicate it," and he said, "I don't care, as long as I get $1.2 million."

Ben and I flipped the place for $1.7 million, and the guy we sold it to flipped it for $2.1 million. There were three settlements in one day on the property. The bank that was lending the money refused to loan because the owner was renting the place to himself for $3 a foot; it had to be at least Master Lease' Ben got back to get the loan.

Ben and I did a master leave, raising the rent to $8 a foot from $3 a foot for five years because it was a five-year balloon, which the bank required for the loan. It cost us $78,000 at settlement, but we got the loan in place and made the deal. Ben and I did several big deals together, and that puts us both back on our way.

The first thing Ben did was buy a plane; the idea was we would fly over land and find land to develop.

I remember when Ben got his plane.

He called me up and said, "I just got my flying license. Let's fly down to Florida."

I said, "Take your girlfriend."

He wanted to fly down the coast, with no radar or anything.

I said, "The weather changes every few hours, and you don't know what you'll run into."

He jumped in the plane with his girlfriend, and they flew down the coast to Florida, down to Miami, and across Florida toward the West Coast. When they got over the Everglades, they ran out of gas, but they saw on the map that there was an airport, which they landed on.

The guy came out, and as he was putting gas in Ben's wing, Ben said, "I don't know if this gas is any good or not."

The man said, "You're not going to leave the plane here overnight, are ya?"

Ben said, "No, why?"

He said, "The gators will crew the tires."

When Bet got back, he called me and said, "I just got back from Florida. Let's go up to Killington, Vermont, and go skiing."

I said okay and we took off. The ride was bumpy up around New York airports, finally, we got to Killington.

The airport was like a bowl because the mountains were five thousand feet high, so we landed and dropped the plane in this bowl. We must have hit the deck at one hundred miles per hour. I thought we were going to blow our tires on the plane.

We left the plane, geared up to go skiing, and we went on top of this mountain. I looked down and it looked like a straight, vertical drop down.

We went down the mountains. I fell down about six times before I finally got to the bottom. I was barely alive, so Ben went and got the car then came and got me.

I said to Ben, "What is the name of this mountain?"

He said, "It's called the Outer Limits."

Then there was another mountain that was like Volkswagen roofs that was called the Cascades.

When we got home, Ben said, "I found the highest waterslide in the world. It's right here in Maryland, let's go this weekend."

So we did. I got on this thing and just closed my eyes when I went down. I remember Ben liked to pretend we were bombing the Cape May Bridge. The plane was a Mooney Executive; it was the fastest single engine plane, at about 350 an hour in a drive.

Ben was a lot younger than me. He was a sea captain, a pilot, a certified skin diver. If it involved any kind of danger, Ben was involved with it.

I remember, Ben had a thirty-seven Hunter sailboat, and he said to me, "Let's sail to Bermuda from Cape May, New Jersey. That's about six hundred miles with no land in between."

I remember we got underway, and it was in June; we got there in four and a half days. The wind was thirty to forty miles per hour all the way there.

I remember I threw up, then Ben threw up, and it was a blowing trip to Bermuda. When we got there, we anchored and went spearfishing the first day. We caught so many fish, we decided to sell them; it was against the law to sell fish in Bermuda without licenses, so we got arrested. We paid a fine and stayed about a week, and then we started back to New Jersey.

On the way back, there was no wind, and we didn't even move. The boat was equipped with a twenty-horsepower Japanese diesel with a forty-gallon tank. We made it all the way back to forty miles off the coast of Cape May and ran out of fuel.

Ben decided to put the dingy, which had a 9.5 Horse Johnson on the bank and put it on the back of the sailboat and pushed it in to Cape May. We arrived at 4:00 a.m. and pulled into a marina. The owner gave us a really hard time about anchoring in the marina overnight, I remember.

When I got out of the service, I thought I was hot stuff; I had been in twenty-eight countries. My brother, Joe, whom we called "Jr.," was ten years older than me. He was a real good-looking guy; he looked a lot like Tyrone Powell.

He called me up one day and said, "Bob, do you want to go to Vegas?" and I said, "Sure, Joe."

And we packed up and went. In those days, you could buy a thousand dollars' worth of chips and get free plane fare for two.

The first time I ever saw Frank Sinatra was on one night that we were in the casino, and I was winning $2,500 on the dice table. In the old days, the old Italian families used to buy Yolanda oil, which was 10 percent olive oil and it was good.

When I rolled the dice, I said, "You seven, you eleven, Yolanda oil $2.79 a gallon."

And Frank Sinatra walked up to me, patted me on the back, and said, "Go get 'em, cumba."

Lucille Ball was betting me on the come, and I said, "Stay with me, reds."

The entire group that later became the Rat Pack was standing around my table that night in the Sands Hotel, Las Vegas.

The second time I saw Sinatra, while we're on the subject, was when I had a coffee shop in a new apartment complex in

Pennsauken, New Jersey—six hundred beautiful apartments. The owner gave me free rent and free utilities if I owned and ran the restaurant there. I had a lot of experience from being raised in my father's diners in my younger years.

The Latin Casino opened up in Cherry Hill, and both head Maître d's lived there. One night, Al Turner, one of the Maître d's asked me if I wanted to go to a birthday party in New York the next day.

I said, "Sure."

He said, "Rent a tux."

We drove up to New York the following day; the birthday party was for Frank Sinatra. He was flying back from the Newport Jazz Festival to do his birthday show in Vegas, and he stopped in New York for this party. I walked in this room at Jillie's, and everybody you could think of was there. Dorothy Killgallon, Mitcey Gainer, Jimmy Durantee, Robert Guilet, Sammy Davis, everyone who was a star was there. Al walked me back to Frank, who was sitting there with his bouncer, and I shook his hand.

I guess the best times I ever had in my life was during that year when I met Al Turner. He was assistant maître d at the Latin Casino in Cherry Hill, and he lived in my building.

I had a penthouse on the top floor, and Al would have all the big stars at the Latin have all their parties in my apartment. I had a corner on the top floor with the river on one side and the pool on the other. I had a balcony that was a Japanese garden. I bought out an estate of a large restaurant owner who went broke. I bought all his oriental furniture, all his teak and ebony, and I had an interior decorator's son decorate my apartment.

I had a glass bar with a pagoda inside and beautiful lights; it was just unbelievable. All the internationally famous stars would come when they played at the Latin. Of course, when Atlantic City opened up, the stars had a sixty-mile radius where they could appear, so the Latin closed up. That was my favorite time of my whole life.

I remember a friend of mine had the limo and parking lot concession at the Latin. My friend would pick me and the girl up and take us to the front door, and then Al would come and seat us, usually down front, near the stage.

I don't remember a better time in my life. I remember one time, Tom Jones was appearing, and we were sitting in what was called the circle seventy ringside, which meant we were in the center touching the stage. Tom Jones came down and said to the girl I was with, "You have beautiful eyes, love." You know you couldn't talk to that girl for three weeks after that.

In those days, it was easy to go into business; I opened my first deli after that. You would rent a store and buy two slicers, two scales, and a cash register. The meat case was free from the meat company, the roll bins were free from the baker, the ice cream cabinet was free from the ice cream company, and they even gave you another one for your frozen food. The milk company gave you your dairy cases, while the grocery company gave you all the shelving, and so on. I set up three delis in those days and sold them for a lot of profit when I finally got out of those businesses.

Today you have to mortgage your house to open a deli. In those days, life was lot simpler, I was a millionaire. I guess all and all, those were the best years of my life. I use to rent a private cabana on the beach in Atlantic City and have a party for the entire weekend, inviting all my friends, and we would have a blast.

Well, you've read about my life. Now I live in a house with my dog; he is a twenty-year-old poodle named Lambchop. When I got my dog, he fit in the palm of my hand. I took Lambchop on my boat, and he loved it. Now he is an old salt like his dad. When I come home, he is always there; nobody loves me like my dog.

Domico and the Savarin Restaurants

Bob Domico took over as general manager of Savarin Restaurants in October. He has already made quite a few changes as far as a new dinner menu, a luncheon buffet Monday through Friday for $2.50 (all-you-can-eat), a Sunday buffet that runs from 2:00 p.m. to 10:00 p.m. for $6.50, including prime ribs, Lobster Newburg, and so on. Also, entertainment for six nights starring Gloria Camfield on Sundays, Mondays, and Wednesdays, and Jackie and Danny Hartman on Thursdays, Fridays, and Saturdays for your dancing pleasure.

Mr. Domico hails from New Jersey, where he managed such distinguished places as Green Valley Country Club. He was director of dining services at Rutgers State University. He owned a 250-seat dinner restaurant. He also owned several delicatessens and a chain of karate schools. Mr. Domico, in the short time that he has been there, has made a lot of friends. A bachelor, he resides in Sterling Park.

Go in and say hello to Bob.

Bill Brewster
The Herndon Tribune

NEW IN NORTH BEACH   North Beach, Md.

DOMICO'S

(Formerly Ewald's Restaurant)

MOTHER'S DAY BUFFET
STEAMSHIP BUFFET
4 Entrees & Salad Bar

$4.95

BIG BAND SOUND

Large Menu
Areas Most
Beautiful
Restaurant At
Areas Lowest
Prices

KALIN TWINS
No Cover   No Minimum
SHOW 8 P.M.

DANCING FROM 5 to 10 P.M.

The Kalin Twins
Million Seller Recording Artists Of The 50

ADVANCE RESERVATIONS PLEASE

Md. 257-3854   D.C. 855-6244

NOW OPEN
Domico's Seafood & Spaghetti House

BOB DOMICO'S LOUISIANA SEAFOOD & SPAGHETTI HOUSE

3901 Mt. Vernon Ave., Alexandria, Va.

MONDAY:
Spaghetti Night! (All You Can Eat)
Domico's famous Italian Spaghetti with Meat Sauce, served with a selection of fresh homemade dressings and Garlic Bread.
All You Can Eat $2.50
Children under 10 $1.25
Children under 6 FREE

TUESDAY:
Shrimp Night – All you can eat!
The Traditional Domico's deep Batter Fried Shrimp, served with French Cole Slaw and Hush Puppies.
All You Can Eat $4.95
Children under 10 $2.50
Children under 6 FREE

WEDNESDAY:
Our Famous Fish Fry (All You Can Eat)
Large Portions of Fresh Fish served with French Fries, Cole Slaw and Hush Puppies.
All You Can Eat $3.25
Children under 10 $1.50
Children under 6 FREE

THURSDAY:
Domico's BBQ Ribs give unbelievable its meats and comes large and hearty.
All You Can Eat $5.95
Children under 10 $2.50
Children under 6 FREE

FRIDAY:
Italian Lovers, Senior Night!
Spaghetti and Meat Balls for Two with Salad, French Bread, and a carafe of Wine.

SATURDAY:
Steak Dinner for Two, Two 8 oz. Delicious Steak Charcoal Broiled with Salad Potatoes, Salad, and Rolls, with a Carafe of Wine to top off the meal.

SUNDAY:
Sunday Special Group Night
$1.00 off on any Platter at our regular meals. Eat it in, or take it home.

PIZZA NIGHT (All You Can Eat)
Children under 10 $1.25
Children under 6 FREE

(All you can eat!)
It's all you can enjoy.

Dart Teams For Summer Leagues Forming NOW
(Dart Boards Available FREE Of Charge)

Thursday Is Ladies' Night
Ladies Get 25% Off All Drinks

Thursday Night Senior Citizens Lunch or Dinner
25% Off All Regular Menu Items

Lunch:
Dinner:
7 Days 11 am -10 pm

Crab House Open April 10th
Crabs Delivered Fresh Daily From
Domico's On The Chesapeake Bay

~Happy Hour~ 25% Off
7 Days 5-7 p.m.   All Drinks

548-5885

Chapter 1

Purchasing an Existing Shopping Center

You see a large complex, which you, of course, would like to own, that's for sale. Maybe it's a shopping center, which has quite a few vacancies. So you go to the realtor and you give him a letter of intent. More on letters, forms, and agreements in another chapter.

After you submit the letter of intent and it is accepted, you place an ad in the newspaper in a large nearby city. The ad will read, "Syndication on 200,000-sq. ft. shopping center, minimum investments $50,000." You will have a meeting every Wednesday night for a month. You will get commitments and deposits from each of the investors.

You will then form a limited partnership with you as the general partner. By doing this, you have control over the whole project. You will put the syndication together and charge 25 percent of their own payment for putting the syndication together.

You will then explain to the group how you intend to fill up the half-empty shopping center. You will go out to all the shopping centers in the area and ask each store owner and franchisee if they would like to expand the operation into another area. You will be seeking the types of business that you need in your shopping center, which you don't have yet. Maybe you need a florist, a pizzeria, a hardware store, etc. You then get involved with the present owners to get a commission or finder's fee for renting the stores for them until your sale is final. Suppose the owners want $2.5 million for the center, but it's worth $4 million fully tenanted. Then the down payment is going to be 20 percent or $500,000. The 25 percent you are charging for the syndication is $125,000, so you need $375,000 from the investors. So if you got ten investors, then you will charge them $37,500 each, plus $12,500 each for your part, for syndicating the deal for them. Another way to do it is if you're already a broker and you list the property; you have a 10 percent commission of $250,000 and you put it in. Now you own 51 percent and have controlling interest in the property.

If you want to get a broker's license, it takes two years in most states. So you take your salesman test and get that license. Then you find an old retired broker and put your license with him and pay him 10 percent of what you get. You, as the general partner of the group, have all the say in the syndication. Once you gain control of the group, you should do an agreement to buy the partners out within the five years after they've received their five years' depreciation.

Use the money you get out of your 25 percent ownership to buy the others out. In five years, you will own the shopping center yourself.

Chapter 2

How to Syndicate a Large Restaurant

You would like to purchase a large restaurant for three million dollars. In most states, you don't need a real estate broker's license to list a restaurant, just file your business brokers company with the local township and get a business license. When you approach the owner to sell his restaurant, tell him that you only charge commission for the business and not the real estate.

The business is worth $1.5 million, and the real estate is worth $1.5 million of the three-million-dollar sales price. The owner will list with you because the commission only costs him half, as opposed to listing with licensed brokers and paying 10 percent of everything. Now the restaurant is listed by you, and it gives you more control of the syndication. Tell the owner when you list it that you intend to syndicate his restaurant.

The people you would contact to syndicate this restaurant with are doctors, lawyers, Indian chefs, and high-income-bracket people who need the write-offs. Remember, a three-million-dollar restaurant has one million dollars' worth of equipment, which can be written off in five years. That's $200,000 write-off a year, which can be passed on to the professional people in the syndication. Tell each person that they get a discount when they have private parties and dinners at their restaurant. Make sure you get three years of books and records to see how much the restaurant is actually netting at the end of the year so you can show the investors.

You will then form a limited partnership, with you as general partner; this will give you control over all the decisions to be made in the group.

The difference between a general partnership and a limited partnership is that in the general partnership, only the general partner is responsible for everything; the most that the limited partner can lose is his investment. Most professional people don't want the exposure. Two of the people in the syndication should be restaurant people who would actually run the restaurant, and maybe an accountant should be brought in the group to keep the books and records for the group. You would be surprised how many people would like to own a restaurant. After you put the group together, you should have a meeting once a month and try to get everybody involved to a certain extent, remembering, of course, that you will have the control and the last say.

You will operate the restaurant for five years and have an option to buy everybody out after five years, after they have received their depreciation on furniture and fixtures. At this point, you will own the three-million-dollar restaurant yourself without putting any money in yourself.

Chapter 3

Putting a Shopping Center Deal Together from Scratch

YOU'RE RIDING DOWN THE highway one day and you see five acres for sale. You inquire and you find out that they are asking $325,000 for the lot. You can envision a fifty thousand-sq. ft. shopping center on the lot; you can close your eyes and see it.

You approach the owner and you offer him the following deal: "If you give me your lot for one year to get approvals to build a fifty thousand-sq.-ft. shopping center on your lot, I'll give you $350,000 ($25,000 more than he is asking) for your lot.

"While getting the approvals on your lot, I will put everything on your desk as I get it. The out bounds, the borings, the traffic count studies, the setbacks, etc., so if for some reason I don't buy your lot, you will be that much closer to approvals if you get the property back, but I must have your lot for a year to get these approvals. McDonald's doesn't buy a lot unless they can put a McDonald's on it."

You sign an agreement with the seller for one year to get approvals on his lot to build a shopping center. You are then going to an engineer to start your project. You tell the engineer that you will pay double his normal fee if he takes the deal on a contingency basis, the contingency being that you get total approvals in a year and sell the project to a developer.

You then go to an architect and do the same deal, then an accountant, and a lawyer; you put your little group together and offer everybody double fees if you sell the project in a year. You can tell them all that this is the first deal, and if everybody works out, you'll be doing lots of deals, and you'll use them for all the other deals too.

The engineer will do your layout, the architect will do the drawings, the lawyer will draw up your papers, and you go to settlement and handle the legal end, and the accountant will do a projected performer showing how much income the center will make and what the expenses will be and what the bottom line will be.

When you get all this information together, you package the whole deal with pictures and figures and then send it out to one hundred developers. Remember, nobody gets paid unless the deal sells. So all the professionals that you're working with will try to sell the package for you. (How many developers do an architect and engineer have in their back pocket?) Let's work the numbers. An approved shopping center is worth about $20 a square foot, unbuilt, without cutting down a tree. Fifty thousand square feet times $20 is a million-dollar selling price to a developer.

You're paying $350,000 for the land, about $15,000 to the engineer, about $38,000 to the architect, $6,000 to the lawyer, and $5,000 to the accountant, which totals roughly $413,000. Your profit is over $500,000 for one year's work. You can do many deals like this at the same time. After you do a couple deals like this, it becomes easier each time.

Chapter 4

Starting Your Own Business Brokerage

AN EASY BUSINESS FOR you to get into is to establish yourself as a business broker; in most states, you don't need a license, just a business license. You can then become a business appraiser, which is very easy, and you can make between $500 and $5,000 for each business that you appraise.

To appreciate a business, you need to get three years of income tax return from the business you're appraising; the income and expense is about a third of the appraisal. The rest consists of income approach, which is putting the amount of profit in a performer as to how much you think the business would make if ran absolutely perfectly.

The next approach is the value approach. You must run comparisons on other businesses in the area that have sold within the last year or so to get a value. And the last approach is the market approach: to check the market for the last year and see how much the other same type businesses have sold in the last year or so.

This is an easy way to make some pocket money to market your bigger deals. Another easy way to make money is to list the property and have the seller purchase his own property. You charge him a small fee for packaging the deal, getting his books and records in order, and going to settlement with him; you can charge him from $1,000 to $10,000 depending on the size of the business.

You could also have an apartment rental business, which rents out for all the large apartment buildings in your area. You advertise in the newspaper, "Apartment for Rent." When the people call, you charge them a fee for doing their application and running a credit report.

You take the people out of your office to several large apartment buildings and charge the apartment buildings one month's rent fee for renting the apartment for them. Being a business broker opens many doors for you to get listings on large businesses so you can syndicate them and have control over the syndication, deciding on who you would like to bring into the syndications.

It's very important to control these syndications you're going to put together. The business brokerage can be used to put you into a situation where you could start syndications, do a couple of small ones, and then jump into a larger deal once you get the hang of it.

List a small business for say, $100,000. Get three guys with $10,000 each. Get the seller to hold a mortgage for say, $75,000 for five years at 8 percent interest. Put down $25,000, find one from the group that will run the operation, and make him the general partner of a limited partnership. He will be responsible for any and all debt that is incurred. The general partner will be responsible for the taxes withheld, paying all the bills, etc. You will charge 25 percent ownership for putting the group together. Plus, you will get the commission for the sale, say 10 percent. This may be what you need to get started in business.

Chapter 5

Highest and Best Use

THE HIGHEST AND BEST use of a building is a fifty-year-old restaurant that's set in the middle of four high-rises. It can be an overdeveloped area with a warehouse in the middle of it or a residential area in the middle of a big commercial area. It can be a closed factory on the river for condo development or a place with great demographics with an inexpensive property in the middle of it.

For an individual to find a property that is not using its highest and best use, one has to use their imagination. Look in areas of an expanding nature and get in the way of development; an expending area is one where development is going in a certain direction and you have to buy in its path.

You have to do the demographics in the area to find out how many people live within five or ten miles of the area. Then find out what the area needs, if there's storage of any sort, and so on. Buy a piece of land bordering a casino. That way, you could expand in the near future. Buy a piece of land next to a cemetery that appears like it's full. Once you become an expert at finding the highest and best use, you can name your own way.

Find the piece of land that is worth a lot more than what sits on it and buy it. Put it into agreements of sale contingent upon getting the highest and best use. The owner will ask what the highest and best use is, say you don't know. You put it into agreements first, then you'll find out what it is. Then after you put it into agreements, you put your syndication together after you decide what the highest and best use is. Then package it and build it or sell the approved site to a developer for about $20 per foot unbuilt.

If you can do a couple of these highest and best use deals, everybody will be breaking your door down to get into the next deal that you do. Once you establish yourself as a successful finder of highest and best use deals, you can make three million a year. Forget the million a year like my book says. You can make more money than doctors, lawyers, and Indian chefs combined, as long as it's not one of the Indian chefs that own one of the casinos up north or out west. Large corporations of developers will be chasing you to offer you a high-paying job.

The highest and best use finder is the highest paid job in the United States. Start studying and learn as much about his angle of work as possible. I can think of fifty properties that are on land that is more valuable than what is on them. How about you?

Chapter 6

How to Purchase a Large Shopping Center

IF YOU WERE A real estate broker, this deal would be easier to do. But let's say you're not. Go out and get a real estate license and offer an old retired broker 10 percent of your commission in a contract.

As a real estate broker, you can find a shopping center for sale and list it and wrap up the whole deal yourself in the following manner. You do not have to have a real estate broker's license to do this deal, but it would help.

You approach the seller and say, "Do you want to sell your property?"

The seller says, "Yes, everything is for sale."

The seller says, "I want two million for my center in my pocket."

You look at the property and it's worth three million dollars easy. You write up the agreement of sale, if you're a broker, for $2.2 million with a ninety-day settlement with a thirty-day extension if, for any reason, either party cannot settle in ninety-days. When you do the agreement, you put in the seller's name as seller and as buyer. You put in your name as nominee or assignee or whatever state you're from for the corporation to be formed.

This gives you the right to assign the agreements to another party and let them pay you a fee for the agreements and go to settlement in themselves. This also gives you the right to syndicate the property by putting an ad in the paper saying, "Syndication of large shopping center, minimum investment of $50,000."

If you're a broker, you can tell the seller that you're syndicating the center and the syndication needs $220,000 or 20 percent to borrow the money from the bank and increase the commission to 20 percent to make the deal fly.

The seller will say again, "I don't care what you do. I just want my $2.2 million."

You then take the next 120 days and market the property. The first thing you should do is contact all the wealthy professional people you know once again, who needs tax write-offs like thirty-year level depreciation on three million; if you're selling the place for three million, it is $100,000 a year to the buyers.

Of course, you're going to advertise your syndication and hope that one guy buys the whole deal so you can walk with $800,000. Of course, if you have to syndicate it, you're only going to wind up owning 25 percent of the deal that you charged to put the deal together. This deal is very easy to do, and you can do it with any type of property, even a house, but remember the center of the deal makes a lot more money.

Chapter 7

Once You Acquire a Large Restaurant

ONCE YOU ACQUIRE A large restaurant, you will need to have a lot of operating capital. My method of acquiring a large amount of cash is the following: You will probably do a million a year in banquet business; this is very important because banquets pay a gratuity of 19 percent, which is $190,000 a year, added on to the bill. If you have a $10,000 wedding, the gratuity is $1,900. This money goes back into the food cost, holding your food at approximately 20 percent so that your gross profit will be about $8,000.

A five-course prime rib dinner will run you about $8 at a wedding. At a wedding, for example, you have 60 percent women and teenagers and 40 percent men. You are charging about $18 per person for liquor, so your liquor cost should be about one dollar per person. If you put in a champagne toast, the wedding cake, the hors d'oeuvres, and a dessert table, you're still ahead of the game.

You would pay your help $15 per hour. A $10,000 wedding would have eight servers, two bartenders, and a maître d at fifteen dollars per hour. That would cost you $825, and the other $1,085 goes back in the food cost, lowering your food cost to 20 percent.

Most of your cash will come from the couple who haven't had their weddings yet. The average bride books her wedding a year ahead of time, so let's say the wedding costs $10,000; the bride is getting married a year from now, so you charge her $800 down and

$800 a month for a year. You don't have to spend the $2,000 that it cost you to do the wedding for a year.

You will have one hundred brides paying you $800 a month. That's $80,000 a month that you don't need for a year. Man, that's cash flow! To keep the people away from the open bar, put carafes of wine on the table; once they start drinking the wine, they'll forget about the bar. As far as the a la carte business, you must train your help to sell to the customer after they come into the restaurant by offering dinner, a drink, an appetizer, an order of sautéed mushrooms for their steak, a bottle of wine, etc.

The low food cost items are 200 to 400 percent profits. You will get the best results by offering a bonus to the person with the highest per-person expenditure for the month. Just have each server add up their total checks for lunch, then divide by the amount of customers; this will give you the per-person expenditure. If a server works twenty days a month, divide by twenty, and this will give you the per-person expenditure for the month. Give the person with the highest per-person expenditure for the month a $250 bonus. Post a chart on the wall, letting them know who is running ahead for the month. Set a standard for all to follow; get your servers into a competitive mode.

To give you an example, let's say you have a fast-food restaurant and your hamburger has a food cost of 50 percent. The French fries are 400 percent profit, the onion rings are 300 percent profit, a large soda is 400 percent profit. The low cost food items are where you make the most money. If you do a million a year, then your side items should average 40 percent of your sales. You will make eight times the profit on the side for low cost food items than you make on the burger. When somebody comes in and orders a hamburger, ask them if they would like large fries or a large soda with that or onion rings or an apple pie.

Have a person come every day and check your liquor behind the bar. You can look at the bottles, 4/10ths, 6/10ths, with your eye and see if there is twenty-eight oz. in a bottle and there are twenty-eight drinks to a bottle, and the bottles on the $3 shelf and the bottles are 5/10ths full, then there should be $42 in the register for that twenty-four-hour period. If you have a cash bar at a banquet, pull out and inventory the bottles, serve the banquet, marry the bottles again after the banquet, and inventory how many full bottles you have to put back in the liquor room in order to establish your liquor cost.

As far as the beer, fill up your beer box at night. It usually holds ten cases or 120 bottles. Keep full and you will always see how much beer you sold, and you will cool the beer overnight rather than cooling in a walk-in box and then moving it into your bar box. As far as doing the inventory for draft beer, if you have ten kegs in tap, you blow one tonight, then you have a 10 percent beer cost. You blow two tomorrows; you have a 20 percent beer cost. You blow zero the third day, you have a 0 percent beer cost. At the end of the week, you divide by seven, and it gives you the beer cost for the week. Always count everything that comes in the back door before the delivery guy leaves.

Chapter 8

Developing a Rural Area Piece of Land

YOU ARE DRIVING DOWN a rural road past some large farms. You see a *For Sale* sign, you approach the farmer, and you ask him how much he wants for his farm.

He says, "A million dollars, how much do you want to pay?"

You say, "I'll give you a million dollars for it under the following terms and conditions."

Remember that the land that's on the highway is improved because you don't have to put a road in to get to it. Approved means it is approved by the township; improved means it's already on a road. (Imagine if the farm was on a corner and you had two road frontages.)

You will create what is called a performance mortgage, meaning you build a house and you pay for the lot. If the farmer has a mile of frontage, he has about thirty-one-acre lots that are already improved.

After you sell off the lots for $80,000 each and pay the farmer off, then you still own the farm and the rest of the land. Now you can lease the farm back to the farmer, run roads in and get all the land approved and sell it to a developer or form a syndication and build it out yourself.

The last thing you're going to do is call the billboard company and put a billboard on each end of the property. You might want to check the zoning map and see if the area is in the commercial or industrial zone or maybe it's in a multiunit zone; it's more valuable if that's the case.

If the farmland falls in the industrial zoning area, then you might want to check in the area for self-storage complexes; it is a very high-yielding business. The cost to build is about $18 per foot, and the return, because you're renting out small spaces, is $18 per foot per year, so you pay the place off in just about a year.

Another warehouse-type use is a commercial mini warehouse, where each man gets a thousand-sq. ft. area with a garage door and a pedestrian door. Small businesses that operate out their home—like plumbers, electricians, or a man who has a store in the mall paying thirty-five dollars a foot—may need a small storage space.

You would get the approvals to build and then send out flyers to all these people and ask their type of business and amount of square footage desired; if you get a hundred thousand sq. ft. of interest letters back, you take that to the bank.

If the bank gives you the money, you build; if not, you syndicate. If you were near an interstate or a large attraction area, you might want to contact the motel chains to build a motel. That is the highest and best use for the land; I'd have to see it to tell you.

Chapter 9

How to Own Many Condos, Collecting Rent without Paying Any Mortgage Payments

I ONCE HAD A friend who purchased twenty condos from a Canadian group, about $30,000 a unit. They were fee simple units that rented for approximately $700 a month each.

My friend owned the properties for ten years and never made a payment on his purchase money mortgage. (A purchase money mortgage is when the seller holds a mortgage.) So my friend collected $14,000 a month rent and only paid the condo fees and the taxes, no mortgage payments. How did he get away with this?

First of all, being fee simple deeds, the large corporation that was based in Canada had to foreclose on them as they became the delinquent, which is very difficult to do. The large corporation was insolvent and could not afford to pay the large legal fees required to do all these foreclosures. The breakdown was it cost him approximately $100 per month for condo fees and $100 a month for property taxes per unit. So his expenses were $4,000 per month, and his profit was $10,000 a month for ten years or $1.2 million.

Understand that he did not have a government-insured mortgage, so he was not defrauding a federal bank; he merely had a mortgage that he was not paying to a large corporation. My friend actually got away with it for ten years. It actually took ten years for the large corporation to foreclose on all twenty of the condos.

When my friend purchased these condos, it was a distressed situation, and he was able to get into the deal with $10,000 down. At settlement, he actually paid the down payment from the proceeds of the security deposits. So basically, he got the whole deal with no down payments and immediately started collecting $14,000 a month rent.

The condo association kept suing my friend for back-condo fees, which he also tried not to pay, but he kept catching them up as they got behind.

The township would keep sending my friend letters of foreclosure and my friend would pay some taxes and not pay other taxes, depending whether they were good tenants in the units or not.

It's possible to do the same thing with a large corporation that were to hold purchase money mortgagers to be able to sell large property or business.

You could actually purchase a large business or piece of real estate and sell it off in pieces like auto parts from a car. Once you purchase the entity, it's very difficult to control the inventory or parts of the company you purchased.

The seller has very little control as to what you do with his company after you take it over. By the time he forecloses on you and gets it back, there's nothing left to salvage.

Chapter 10

Developing Raw Land and Making It Very Valuable

A PIECE OF LAND has four values:

The present value of the land. To determine this, search the comparable in the area to see what similar pieces of land size wise and similar zoning pieces of land have sold for in the recent year. Once you establish value, then you can establish the four values. Say the present value of the five-acre land is $300,000.

If you decide to put a shopping center on the property, say fifty thousand sq. ft., and if you get it approved, it's worth about $20 a square foot unbuilt without cutting down a tree. Say one million dollars.

Value is if you get it approved and you build it out; it's worth about $80 a square foot or about four million.

Value if it's rented out is worth $100 per foot or five million dollars depending where you are with it. Remember that once you put the deal in contract, you have total control over the property as long as you do everything the contract says.

Say you wanted to build an industrial park, an office building or an apartment building, the same situation applies. The basic fundamentals apply in deals where you are starting with raw land.

Again, as in chapter 3, you will approach the owner of the land and ask him if he wants to sell his land. Promise to put the approval papers on his desk as you receive them from the township, and use your architect, engineer, accountant, and attorney on a contingency where you pay them double if they wait for you to sell the deal.

Remember, you can sell the land and the deal anytime, or get it approved and sell it, or build it and sell it, or build it and rent it out and sell it at any time and at any of the four values you can sell. You can also keep the property for rent and collect rent for the rest of your life and have the tenants pay off your mortgage for you.

Remember to go through what's called a property inspection checklist. Location/area: area economy, job availability, growth potential; schools' quality, types, locations, distance; freeways; nearest access, convenient routes, transit, nearest bus or train shop; parks and recreation; cultural facilities: churches, neighborhood economy: growth or decline; fire or police stations; predominate zoning pattern; is there change? streets and roads: is maintenance adequate? snow removal; trash collected.

Once you do one or two deals, you'll be pretty much set. The whole idea is to get started and go through this exercise with unwavering courage and mastery of detail. Remember to follow through this exercise with unwavering courage and mastery of detail. Remember to follow through and do not give up until the deal is finished. A trip of a thousand miles starts with the first step.

Chapter 11

Proven System to Purchase Houses and Have Your Tenants Pay Off the Mortgages for You

IN MY YOUNGER DAYS (much younger days), I had a friend who was working down south and ran into some VA assumable mortgages. He had a good job; he was making $37,000 a year in the early seventies, so he went around trying to purchase as many of these assumptions as he could. Most of them were 6.5 or 7 percent so that the mortgage payments were about $450 per month, and he rented them out for an average of about $850 per month.

He was very close to Washington, where people from all over the country came to work. The people were there for three or four years and then they would move on to another area. The turnover in the Washington area caused a 20 percent a year in appreciation, so if you held on to a property for five years, it would double in value.

He would approach the owner, who was just about to be transferred, and offer them four or five thousand to take over their mortgage; occasionally, he would sell a property to create more cash to buy more real estate.

He managed to acquire twenty houses, which doubled in value after five years. Say you put $5,000 in the bank at 7 percent interest; you're going to make $350 a year interest. Say you take that same

$5,000 and put it down on a house. If the house is worth $100,000 when you purchased it and it appreciates 10 percent a year, it's worth $120,000 in a year. Say your tenant pays the mortgage for you after you put a hundred in your pocket every month. Instead of the 7 percent from the bank, you made more than 22 percent interest.

The VA assumptions kind of wore off in the eighties, but there are still plenty out there to be had, especially if someone assumed a loan, and now you can assume it from them. If they can't pay the mortgage anymore, you can offer them less down and have them hold a second mortgage.

Governmental loans are all assumable, unless they say that they're not. For example, SBA (Small Business Administration) loans are assumable if you want to take over someone's business.

When you take out a government loan, if you pay a couple of extra points, you can make it assumable. You don't have to move to Washington to do this, just check the areas around the United States where the appreciation is high.

Chapter 12

Hot to Put a Casino Deal Together

I GOT INTERESTED IN the casino business when an old client called me one day and said he was building a casino in Atlantic City and he wanted me to sell it for him.

The casino he was building was a big rental situation. In other words, the casino would be rented to a casino operator, the parking garage would be rented to a parking garage company, the restaurants would be rented to a restaurant company, and so on.

The man wanted me to find these tenants for him to put this deal together, and he would pay me one million dollars for this effort.

I got several tenants interested in renting from the man, but he was never able to put the financing together to build the casino even with my tenants in place. He probably would have put the deal together, but we happened to be in a bad market that year.

The next opportunity to put another casino deal together was when I got a call from a man in Long Island, New York, who had purchased a condominium project that didn't sell out. There were three hundred units built, mostly for the casino employees, where only about thirty units sold.

Across the street was a quality inn that was owned by another client of mine where he was asking $18 million for the hotel. I checked with the casino commission board, and you had to have, at the time, five hundred rooms, 25,000 sq. ft. of gambling area and ample parking.

I had an architect draw a picture of the condominium project with a bridge crossing over to the quality inn across the street to make six hundred rooms, then I took a section of the garage to make 25,000 sq. ft. of gambling area. Then under the bridge, I had to draw two other casinos that were next door. The whole picture was beautiful. I then went to Nevada. I started in Las Vegas and drove the whole state all the way up to Reno and Lake Tahoe to show my drawing to every mom-and-pop casino operation in the state of Nevada. But again, my efforts were lost. Instead of spending three hundred million dollars for a casino, they could have put this one together for under one hundred million.

The third casino deal I tried to do was when the Sands and the Clearage Casinos went into bankruptcy; I tried to put a deal together to combine and bridge the two smaller casinos together and make one large casino. Somebody gave me a drawing of an Asian casino that all the dealers, the waiters, the bartenders—everybody—in the casino were Asian. The food was Asian, the whole casino design inside and out was Asian, so I tried to market the package like it was on the drawings.

I guess you have to be in that loop to be able to put those kinds of deals together because I never could.

Another Atlantic City deal I worked on for about eight years was with a client of mine who purchased a large piece of marshland coming into Atlantic City, filled it in where he had one hundred acres of uplands to build ten non-casino hotels, a large shopping mall, ten casino billboards, and five fast-food restaurants. The property was two minutes away before you got to Atlantic City on the expressway.

He wanted to contact the existing casinos to have a non-casino hotel that would be connected to the casinos and operated by the casinos in Atlantic City. The project had a giant parking lot in it, which was to be opened to casino customers and then be used into the casinos.

Another casino deal I tried to put together was to take a large ship and to make it into a casino. The USS United States was docked in Philadelphia. I called the owners, and they said they wanted ten million dollars for it. The country of Ireland was willing to donate thirty-seven acres of waterfront land in Southern Island for economic development to create jobs for the people. I put about a year on that deal but found out it was too expensive to convert a three-thousand-suite ship into a casino.

Asian casino with Asian dealers, Asian cocktail waitresses, etc., for Asian customers and everybody else.

This diner was built by Robert Domico when he was twenty-six. It was a sixty-foot Paramount Diner and a sixty-five foot Mountain View Diner put in an L shape, all the stainless steel removed and covered with brick.

Casino Mall: gambling concession, parking lot, franchise restaurant chain, and other concessions all to be rented out.

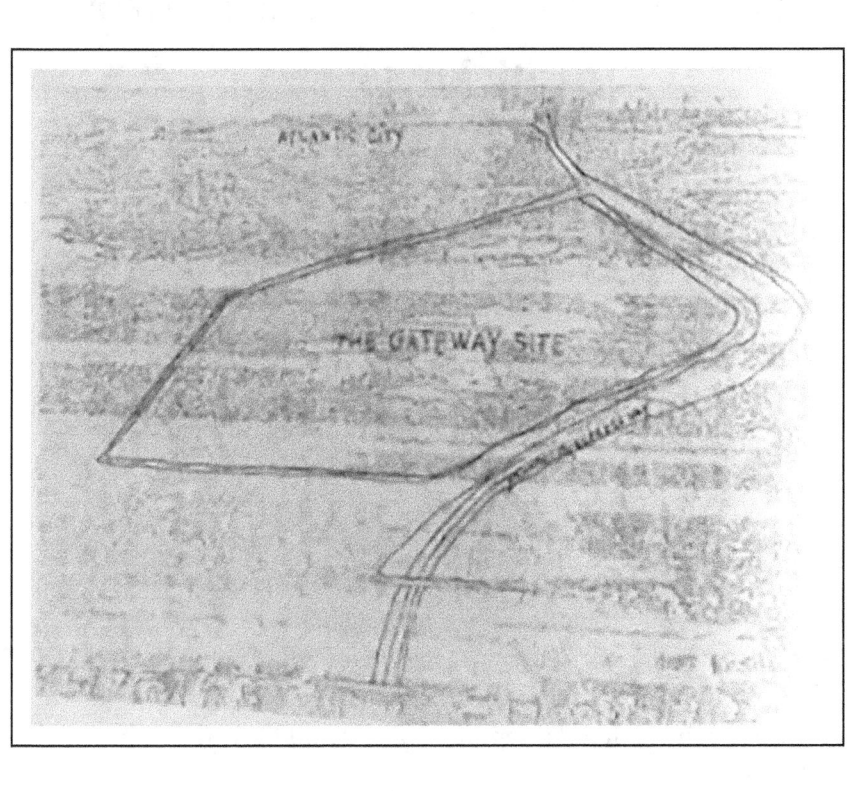

Chapter 13

How to Pull Money out of Real Estate, with No Money

A SHOPPING CENTER IS for sale for $600,000; it's worth $1,000,000, so you get the appraisal on it for $1,000,000. The mortgage company will lend you eighty percent LTV (loan to value) of the appraised value, so they will lend you $800,000. You paid $600,000, so you put $200,000 in your pocket with no investment.

The tenants on the shopping center will pay ample rents to cover the price of the mortgage payment. The tenants will go on to pay off the entire mortgage in time.

You don't have to pay capital gain taxes because you borrowed the money; you did not earn the money.

On a smaller scale, I sold a friend of mine a property that I foreclosed on with a tax sale certificate. I had about $80,000 that I invested in it, it was appraised at $250,000, and I sold it for $160,000.

My friend borrowed 80 percent of the appraised value, which was $200,000. My friend put $40,000 in his pocket. He then rented out the property, and the tenant paid off the loan for him. Again, he did not pay capital gains taxes because he did not earn the money; he borrowed it.

With this newfound money, you can go to sheriff sales and purchase deals for 50 or 60 percent of what their worth and put 20 or 30 percent money for your pocket by borrowing 80 percent of the LTV.

Never ever spend any of the money that you are making because it's in your pocket until you're so far ahead that it doesn't make any difference anymore. If you spend all your money, then you're out of the business again, and then you have to start all over. You will be apt to spend your money, especially, if you never had that kind of money before in your pocket.

The old families in the United States who bought the real estate never sold it. They just kept buying and buying and then passed it down to their children, from generation to generation, and real estate always went up in value.

Presently, the real estate market is very bad; it is an opportunity to purchase real estate at tremendously low prices. People are running scared. It's the time to buy; it's a buyer's market. Now is the time to make your deals, so get out there and start looking hot and heavy because when things get better, people don't have to sell if it's harder to buy.

Chapter 14

How to Own 51 Percent of a Law Firm and Create a Million-Dollar Equity in a House

A FRIEND OF MINE recently bought a tax sale certificate and foreclosed on this large house that was next door to a courthouse in South Jersey. My friend remembered on a recent trip down south to Virginia and Maryland that wherever there was a courthouse, there were law firms all around it.

My friend went to court there to see what went on. He saw ten DWIs, about twenty speeding tickets, and a half-dozen domestic affairs in the court that night.

My friend realized that if a couple of young lawyers were to rent next door, they would have thirty cases a week from that courthouse.

My friend decided to make his recent acquisition—a law firm. There were no lawyers in this small town at the time. He went in to a township meeting and got a variance from residential to professional zoning. It was only one upgrade from residential; two upgrades would have been commercial zoning, which he didn't need.

He then pulled out the two bathrooms and made them powder rooms, tore out the kitchen and made it a conference room, and then had seven more rooms for offices.

He took off the enclosed porch and made a nice Victorian open porch with spindled railing and Victorian trim. He took away the fence and did beautiful landscaping.

Now instead of making a house out of it and bringing in $1,500 a month, he now had a property that would rent out for $14 per foot by 2,500 feet equals $35,000 a year income. Using a ten percent capitalization rate, now the property is valued at $350,000.

My friend wasn't satisfied with $350,000 value he created, so he decided to form a limited partnership with two young lawyers right out of Law Rodgers Law School and now owns 51 percent of a law firm.

Last year, my friend netted $122,000 for his 51 percent interest in the law firm. Now using a 10 percent capital rate again, the property as an income property is worth 1.2 million dollars.

You see how easy it is to create equity until you get the zoning changed. Put it in the agreements when you purchase the property "contingent on the commercial zoning." McDonald's doesn't buy a lot unless they build a McDonald's on it.

Remember that commercial zoning is worth $14 per foot, rather than $1,500 a month if it were a house instead. Since my friend built this law firm contiguous to City Hall, two more lawyers opened up law firms across the street in empty stores that were not even rented before.

Chapter 15

How to Flip Large Properties without Actually Purchasing Them

I ONCE WENT INTO agreements on a very large property; it was a large shopping center that was owned by a large lumber company. The shopping center was sixty thousand sq. ft. and the owner leased 24,000 sq. ft. for himself, for his lumber company, and for his home improvement center.

I went up to the owner and asked him how much he wanted for his center, and he said $1.2 million. Well, I thought right away that was too cheap.

I was a real estate broker at the time, so I said, "I'll list your property and then I'll syndicate it."

He agreed and we signed the papers.

I went back to the owner the following week and told him that he had to pay me a 20 percent commission because I was syndicating it and the bank required 20 percent down payment.

He said, "I don't care, I just want $1.2 million for it."

He agreed and the commission became 20 percent.

I then decided to go into agreements myself with the owner, which gave me a lot of control over the deal, I put the deal into agreements for $1.2 million net, then I added on the 20 percent commission, which brought the price up to $1.440 million.

I found a buyer in a couple of weeks and went into agreements with him for $1.8 million. When the new buyer went in for financing, he found out that the owner was leasing to himself for $3 per foot. We had to do a master lease for the bank for $8 a foot so they would finance it, which we did. We had to pay the difference for $5 per foot by 2,400 sq. ft. for five years because it was a five-year balloon. It cost us $60,000 at settlement.

The buyers flipped the property again for $2,200 so that on the day of the settlement, there were three settlements in three different rooms. Of course, the middle buyer had to pay the capital gains taxes for the original seller.

It turned out to be a great day for everyone concerned; everybody made money that day. It's easy to find underpriced properties to flip. You just have to keep looking for them and keep going into agreements with properties. You can control real estate without purchasing it. As long as you do everything on that agreement of sale, you have total control of that property.

It's also easy to do an assignment agreement. You would go into agreements of sale and then assign the agreements to another party. You would do an assignment agreement with your buyer and let them go to settlement.

You want to tie up the property for at least ninety days with a thirty-day extension. If for any reason either party cannot settle, that will give you 120 days to sell the property, flip the property, syndicate the property, or assign the property to another buyer.

To syndicate a property, you just put an ad in the paper saying, "Syndication on shopping center, minimum investment of $50,000." You then have a meeting every Wednesday night at 8:00 and sit around a large table, usually a conference room in someone's office. You then form a limited partnership and collect 20 percent from everyone that comes in and the balance at settlement.

You would then put the financing together, or it might be owner financed, then the owner/seller becomes the bank. The advantage is that the seller, instead of getting cash and paying high capital gain taxes, gets whatever you raise from your syndication down and pays the taxes as he receives the money over time; that's called installment taxes. Now the owner gets more money for his place because of his interest.

Chapter 16

How to Syndicate

DID YOU EVERY LOOK at a building and say, "Boy, if I had that building, I wouldn't have to work anymore?" Well, that building is easier to get than you think. You go in and put that building into agreements with the owner and tell the owner that you are going to syndicate his building, and he will be paid in full for his building in 120 days.

When you do your agreement of sale, make sure you word it in the following manner. Your name and the state you're in, say New Jersey, corporation to be formed or nominee or assignee, hereafter known as "buyer," and the seller's name, hereafter known as "seller."

Whereas the seller wishes to sell and the buyer wishes to buy that certain land and building known as 300 N. Broadway Camden, New Jersey, and known on the tax map in the city of Camden as lot no., block no., and so on.

This wording will enable you to syndicate the property to assign the property by forming an LLC and putting the deal together in whatever way you see fit.

After the owner signs the agreement of sale and you have him tied up for 120 days, you can start advertising for your syndication in the newspaper. Your ad will read, "Syndication on large office building, minimum investment of $50,000."

The person will call you and you will have a meeting, say every Tuesday night at eight o'clock. You will sit down with your prospective investors and get a 10 percent deposit, the balance due on the day of settlement.

You will show the person the books and records showing income and expense on the property. You will convince the person that it is a good investment, secured by real estate. Then you will show the person what kind of return he or she will expect to get back every year.

The general partner in a limited partnership will have a lot to say about how the corporation is run. As a general partner in a limited partnership, they will be responsible for all the liabilities of your partnership, such as taxes due, withholding of the employees' (if any) the taxes due to the government, and the state taxes due.

When you form this limited partnership, make sure that you leave yourself in there. Set up an agreement that you can buy out the other partners in there. Set up an agreement that you can buy out the other partners in five years after the depreciation on furniture and fixtures is over.

You might want to sell the property after five years, but first you have to own it. So set up the syndication where you can buy it out, after all it's your syndication.

This syndication is easy to do, but whatever you do, don't let the general partner ever have the power to buy you out.

You can charge 25 percent ownership in the syndication for finding the deal and putting it together. Some will have a hard time swallowing that, but if they wanted to join your group, they have to give it up.

What you're going to do is have a good plan that works, besides being secured by real estate. You must prepare for a good performer to show the income and expense sheet for the first five years as to how much money the syndication will make.

It's good to ask the seller of the property for five year's income tax returns even if they don't show that much; read between the lines and keep an open mind.

Chapter 17

The 1031 Exchange

FREQUENTLY ASKED QUESTIONS (FAQ) about 1031 Exchanges

What is a 1031 exchange?

Under Internal Revenue Code (IRC) Section 1031, a real property owner can sell certain property and then reallocate the proceeds in ownership of like-kind property and defer the capital gains taxes. To qualify as a like-kind exchange, property exchanges must be done in accordance with the rules set forth in the tax code and in the treasure regulations. The 1031 exchange can offer significant tax advantages in real estate buyers.

Who should consider 1031 exchange?

If you have real property that will net you a gain upon sale (generally, property that has been substantially depreciated for tax purposes and/or has appreciated in fair market value), then you are exactly the person who should consider a 1031 exchange.

There are five tax classes of property:

1. Property used in taxpayer's trade or business
2. Property held primarily for sale to customers
3. Property that is used as your principal residence

4. Property held for investment
5. Property used as a vacation home

Section 1031 applies to the first and fourth categories and sometimes the fifth category. Business use is defined as "to hold property for productive use in trade or business." Property retired from previous productive use in business can be qualifying property. Investment purpose is defined as a real estate, even if unproductive, held by a non-dealer for future use, or the increment in value is held for investment and not primarily for sale. Investment is the passive holding of property for more than a temporary period, with the expectation that it will appreciate. Property held for sale in the immediate future is not held for investment.

Why should you consider a 1031 exchange?
Defer paying capital gains taxes. A properly structured exchange can provide real estate buyers with the opportunity to defer all or most of their capital gains taxes.

Leverage.
Upgrade or consolidate property.
Diversify.
Own multiple properties rather than just one.
Relocation to a new area.
Differences in regional growth or income potential.
Change property types among commercial, retail, etc.

What are the general 1031 exchanges?
The real property you sell and the real property you buy must both be held for productive use in a trade or business or for investment purposes and must be like-kind.
The proceeds from the sale must go through the hands of a qualified intermediary and not through your hands or the hands of one of your agents or else all the proceeds will become taxable.

All the cash proceeds from the original sale must be reallocated to the replacement property—any cash proceeds that you retain will be taxable.

The replacement property must be subject to an equal level or greater level of debt than the relinquished property or the buyer will either have to pay taxes on the amount of the decrease or have to put in additional cash funds to offset the lower level of debt in the replacement property.

Disclaimer: There are substantial risks associated with the federal income tax consequences of purchasing and owning real estate properties especially if the purchase is part of a tax-deferred exchange under section 1031 of the code. In addition, the income tax consequences of purchasing and owning real property are complex. And because the tax consequences are complex and certainty of the tax consequences may differ depending on individual tax circumstances, each prospective purchaser must consult with and rely on his own independent tax advisor, concerning the tax consequences of such purchase and his individual situation.

The 1031 Exchange

A 1031 exchange is an exchange of property in which capital gains tax deferral is available to real estate owners who sell their investment, rental, or business real estate and reinvest the proceeds in qualified replacement properties. The replacement property must be similar in nature (to be used for investment, rental, or business) and therefore considered "like-kind."

Property owners may sell and replace like-kind properties and defer taxes on the profits by meeting the requirements of Internal Revenue Code (IRC) for 1031 exchange properties.

Sellers of 1031 exchange properties have a maximum of 180 calendar days from the closing of the initial sale of the relinquished property to complete the exchange into their replacement properties. Within the first forty-five days of after the close, a seller must designate replacement property and properly identify them in compliance with IRS's regulations. This is most frequently done by using a qualified intermediary, also known as an exchange of accommodator.

There are three rules for identifying replacement properties for a 101 tax exchange. The most common is the three-property rule, which states that a seller may identify up to three replacement properties regardless of their value. The second rule is that a seller may identify any number of replacement properties, but the combined value may not exceed 200 percent of the value of the initial property sale. The third rule for identifying replacement properties is a number of properties of any value may be identified as long as the final value of the properties exchanged is equal to 95 percent of all the replacement properties identified. The funds in a trust account with the qualified intermediary can be used as deposit or earnest money in the purchase of the designated replacement property once all IRS requirements for a 1031 exchange are met.

If no new properties are identified in the first forty-five days and no designated transaction is completed during the dull 180-day period, the funds in the trust account will be liquidated and the sale proceeds taxed at the prevailing state and federal capital gains and depreciation recapture taxes.

Many investors don't take advantage of the 1031 exchanges because of the fear of the forty-five-day identification period. This fear is supported by numerous horrors stories of failed exchanges and the devastating taxes that can result from such failures.

With proper planning and the right resources, investors can navigate the waters of a 1031 exchange and frequently double or triple their investment income while diversifying their portfolio thus reducing risk. Key requirements are a good grasp of the exchange process, a clear set of involvement objectives, and a plenty and consistent source of quality replacement properties.

Chapter 18

How to Set Up a Web Page to Advertise Your Syndication Business

You want to set up your web page so you can get interested partners for your syndications. You want to advertise that you do syndications on large pieces of real estate, large business, etc. Maybe you've established a business brokerage by now or even become a tax sale certificate dealer.

Whatever you decide to do with your time, it's good to have a web page to advertise on. When I decided to have a web page, I got a Verizon Yellow Pages to design my web page with colored pictures and beautiful designs and wordings. They included my web page with my yellow-page advertisement in the phone book at one low price.

You want to advertise exactly now, you syndicate your deals with not a lot of details, you don't want someone else picking up exactly what you're doing and copying it. You'll mention that you do a partnership, don't say what kind, and that you choose your partners according to their experience and skills, and they must qualify for the group.

Although you will get most of your partners out of the newspaper, it's always good to have a web page so you can identify to the public exactly what it is that you do.

You will advertise that you put these syndications together, elaborate on the tax advantages and the fact that they own a part of the syndication, and that the group deal is secured by real estate, which makes it a very safe investment.

If you start three or four of these deals all at once, you will quickly gain experience and an experience level you'll find that the same people will come back into your deals over and over once you establish yourself as a proven person that syndicates deals successfully.

In your web page, you could show a couple of deals that you're working on to try to get people interested in your syndications. You will have the big questions and answers for the meetings, where you meet with four or five potential partners at once. At those meetings, you want to get rid of the instigators, the people who ask for too many answers at once and try to push you to the limit at every meeting.

They have to understand that you're putting this syndication together for everyone's mutual benefit and that sometimes syndications have their ups and downs, especially when you take a bunch of people and put them together in a deal for the first time.

Save the details for the meetings: the type of partnership it is, that the group must choose a general partner, and that the group will be responsible for voting that partner in and out it it's necessary.

Chapter 19

How to Take Useless Land and Make It Very Valuable

A FRIEND OF MINE purchased five hundred acres on the Atlantic City expressway, about two minutes before you arrive in Atlantic City.

It was a wetland and primarily useless. He then hired one of the best environmental attorneys he could find and got one hundred acres of uplands approved; after filling in with dirt and from the bay floor next door, he raised the one hundred acres about a foot of elevation.

He then went in for approvals for five hotel sites (2,500 rooms), a fashion mall of five hundred sq. ft., five fast-food restaurants, a large day-care center, five casino billboards, and moving the large adjacent—owned by the DOT—2,500 car parking lot on to his property.

My friend made a deal with the department of transportation to make two exits on his property from the expressway and one exit from the adjoining town onto his property and got the DOT to pay for all the new roads.

The deal turned out to be a $250-million build-out. His intention was to get everything approved and then sell the project to a developer. He was not able to sell the deal, but what a deal it would have been.

Atlantic City is located on Absecon Island, which is approximately six square miles; another piece is Beater Field, which is fifty acres, presently marked for development. And here sits my friend's one hundred acres, still now developed.

My friend once told me a story, how he purchased one thousand acres of landlocked land for $200 per acre and then bought an easement to get to it for $250,000 and built a huge development.

He told me that they were building a beltway around Atlantic City Airport and gave me a map with an overlay of where the new airport expansion was going to be, and he told me to purchase the land around it to make hotel sites in all the right places to get approved and sell off to developers.

These stories are kind of like the movie Superman, where Lex Luthor is dropping a bomb on San Andreas Fault and making a new San Francisco right next to it, on land that he already purchased.

With Atlantic City expanding and building more casinos, it's just a matter of time before someone comes and develops this piece. I wish my friend had done it; he was a good man. Las Vegas is one of the hottest developing areas in the United States. Of course, we are in a bit of a recession now. There are many ways to bring undeveloped land into fruition; you just have to make the effort and make sure it's timely.

Chapter 20

More Development of Useless Empty Land

ANOTHER FRIEND OF MINE decided to put under option a large piece of land on the river next to a large oil refinery. I remember going on the land and seeing deer drinking from a stream and this beautiful large piece of land with lots of environmental problems. The land had swamped pig, bog turtles, green moss on the rocks, and Indian burial ground, a bird path; you name it, it was there.

My friend tried to get homes approved, detached or semidetached, apartments, condos, a large shopping center, a large professional complex, and five hundred boat slips with a huge boat shopping mall for boat buyers. He wanted to put a ferryboat service in because Philadelphia was across the river; you could live here and not take your car to work, jump on a ferryboat instead.

Finally, he got preliminary approvals enough to start trying to market the approved site. Remember the retables of a township is very important; those extra taxes the town would get with a development like this will turn any city government around. So he drew up conceptual drawings, renderings of what it would look like; he did boring pictures of the finished development, projected performer as to income and expense, profits—the whole nine yards. He then packaged it and showed it to thirty different large developers; still, he was unable to market the project.

So he decided to market the project overseas. He first brought in the Japanese. I remember the day he had these Japanese people come and look at the land; they arrived by helicopter and landed right in the middle of the land. They knew after doing some preliminary studies that the idea was too new for the area.

After that, he showed the properties to four other foreign countries and always the same conclusion occurred. The area just wasn't ready for this project size.

There was nothing wrong with the plan; it was just too immature, too new. The area wasn't quite ready for this big of a project. Today, twenty years later, someone came along and actualized my friend's idea. Of course, now it's an over-fifty-five community, plus everything else my friend planned for the development including the boat slips.

It is very important to run the demographics on an area to determine the need—how many people are within a ten-mile radius, is it a moving area, are things happening? Don't get trapped into believing that you can make everything happen yourself.

Investigate the job market in the area, see if there are any large facilities being built or coming into the area that will employ thousands of people, and check and see what the appreciation of real estate has been in recent years; do your due diligently.

Once you get the idea, go into agreements with the company that's selling the property. Start to market the idea. Put an ad in the Wall Street Journal, which says, "Large development, three hundred million-dollar build-out minimum investment of $50,000 a share." Then determine how many shares it takes to put this deal together. Price the deal out and see how much it will cost to build it out.

A deal like this takes a lot of work, but if you hit on it, that's all you need. One successful deal like this and you're home free. You can take it easy for the rest of your life.

Chapter 21

How to Develop an Over-Fifty-Five Community

As far as approvals for this type of development, it's probably the easiest to get. Imagine if you were a township and someone came into your office and proposed a deal where the owners of the property paid taxes to the township but didn't have any kids in school. The township would welcome you with open arms.

You find a piece of land large enough to put one hundred units and over fifty-five communities on. You put the deal in contract, contingent upon putting an over-fifty-five community on the land. You tell the owner that you must get approvals for the deal to go through. You tell the owner that if the approvals are received, you will purchase his land for an agreed price.

You tell the owner that you will enter into agreements with him, contingent upon getting the approvals on an over-fifty-five community once you get the approvals and you sell the approved site to a developer, unless you decide to build the development yourself. The owner must agree to give you the property for one year to get it approved. You can offer the owner the full price he is asking if he agrees to do this.

You will then enter an engineer's office and propose to him that if he does all the engineering for you, when you sell the deal or build it yourself, you will pay him double. This is for waiting for the money. You then need an architect to draw up the plans for you; same deal, he gets paid when you sell it or build it yourself. Then he also gets paid double for waiting for his money.

Now you need an attorney to draw up your papers and handle the settlement for you. He also will get paid double to come. The accountant you need will draw up a projected performer for you, showing income and expense and what the project will make in profits should you build the project out yourself and also to show the group what you put together, should you decide to syndicate the project. Again, he gets paid when you do something with the project, again double.

How you're going to put everything on the seller's desk as you receive it—engineering, architect's plans, projected performer from the accountant, everything you've done—in case you don't go through with the deal, the owner will have most of the paperwork done for him, making the property more valuable.

If you decide to build the property out yourself, then you will need money. So it becomes necessary to do syndication in the following manner: You will put an ad in the large newspaper, like the Wall Street Journal or the Hong Kong Times saying, "Investors syndication over fifty-five communities in—." Then describe the location that you want to build the project in. "Minimum investment of $50,000, unbelievable returns and write-offs to the investors."

As you receive your calls from your advertisement, arrange a meeting to sit down with your investors to tell them the advantages of investing in you project. Speak to your accountant to show you the advantages of tax write-offs and depreciation write-offs, and so on, so you can show the investors this investment is secured by real estate.

At this point, you'll want to form a limited partnership; have your accountant do that too. Name yourself as the general partner, responsible for all the losses in the group, and assure the investors that the most he can lose is his investment, but that's not probable.

Put yourself for 25 percent ownership in the syndication, and don't let anyone bully you out of that. Ask for a 10 percent deposit to hold the investors' position at the meeting so that you can move forward.

Have an option in the paperwork that you can buy your partners out after five years, after they've received five years of depreciation. Take the money out of your personal profits in the deal to buy out your partners.

This is a typical deal that you can put together with no money; all you need is one of the deals.

Chapter 22

How to Put Together a Trailer Park

FIND A TWENTY- OR thirty-acre piece of land on the outskirts of town where you can get approvals for a trailer park. Again, go into agreements with the seller contingent upon getting approvals on a trailer park; you're going to need the land for about a year to get approvals.

Go to the township and check the zoning map for residential zoning, hopefully with multi-dwelling; otherwise, you'll have to get variance for that use. Go to an engineer again and have him do a deal with you that if you sell the project or build it yourself, you'll pay him double if he waits for his money.

Once again, get your lawyer and architect involved, getting paid to come if you sell the approved project or you build it out yourself. You will want a clubhouse to entice the residents to come into your park. You want a meeting place, a place to have functions and parties and social events so they can interact with each other, and a swimming pool to bring the neighbors together. The more activities, the better the park.

The best trailer park, and easiest to get approved, is an over fifty-five community park. Once again, they pay taxes but don't have anyone in schools. The trailer park is a good source of income. After all, you're not building buildings; you're just renting lots for about $500 a month—not bad.

You can create a nice capitalization rate with a trailer park; it's worth many times what you put into it. Let's see now, you purchase a piece of land for say half a million. Let's say you get one hundred lots on the land. Let's say it cost you by the time you put the well and septic systems in, roads, and everything, you need a total of one million dollars. Let's say you take in one hundred by $500 a month, that's $50,000 a month or $600,000 per year income.

Your debt service on the million is about $120,000 a year; add labor and maintenance, you still won't reach $200,000 a year expenses. So that's about $400,000 a year net operating income. That makes your investment using a 10 percent capitalization rate worth about four million dollars for your one million-dollar investment.

How come when you form your syndication you have something that's easy to sell? You won't have the type of write-offs that you'll have on your regular buildings, but look at your income.

Now you're ready to do your syndication again, put ads in the newspaper asking for your investors to invest in a trailer park. Use a large newspaper to advertise as the larger the newspaper, the more people will call. "Minimum investment of $50,000." Then you're going to get an economic development loan for low-income housing to build your park. This is a sure-fire retirement plan for you, if you can pull it off.

Trailer parks are best built off resort areas because besides people renting in them locally, you have an element that will have a second home near a resort area, maybe near the shore or near a country club or a mountain resort.

Wherever you put one, it will do well in bad times or good times, neither affects this market.

Chapter 23

Building a Marina with Very Little Waterfront: The New Wave

FIND A PIECE OF land, maybe five acres that has about fifty feet of waterfront. Make sure you have Riparian rights for that fifty feet of waterfront. You're going to need a fifty-foot-long, two-sided floating dock. Then look into purchasing five large boat stackers that will accommodate twenty boats each. This will allow you to have one hundred boats on your property, push whatever other boats you can store on the balance of the land.

You're going to need a building about five thousand sq. ft. for your repair shop and a forklift to drop the boats in and pull them out of the water. The land should be mostly asphalt with adequate parking for about fifty cars.

The idea is that the boat owner calls up and says, "I'll be down at the marina at 2:00 p.m." and you'll take the forklift, go to the boat stacker, take his boat, and put it in the water to have it ready when he gets there. When he comes back, you get the forklift again and put it back on the boat stacker's rack.

You should be able to get about 125 boats for storage at about $1,500 per boat, that's $187,500. The repair work on the boats should bring another $200,000; with new boat sales and parts, it should bring another $200,000 per year. It's a good business that would net about $150,000 to $200,000.

Using a 10 percent capitalization rate, the business and property will be worth $1.5 million to $2 million.

You don't need a building site; you can use wetlands for your site with enough upland to build your five thousand sq. ft. boat repair building, which could be a pole building or an inexpensive steel building, allowing you to create a valuable property for very little money. Remember, you don't need a permanent dock, just a floating dock.

You should be able to use wetlands for this type of use because there is no permanent use here; you might have to put stones on the land for parking so that the water flows through.

Again, to put this deal together, you have to syndicate it. Put your ad in saying, "For syndication on marina, minimum investment of $50,000." You might want to advertise in a boating magazine or a boat newspaper.

Form a limited partnership with you as the general partner. It's not the biggest deal in the world, but maybe it's something you've been thinking about for a while and just didn't know how to go about it.

Remember, you are the general partner, and if you run the operation, you'll also get a salary.

Chapter 24

How to Build a Floating Home Park

THERE ARE VERY FEW floating home parks in the United States, as far as I know, one in New Jersey and another one in California. However, it's a good deal as far as the numbers go, and you might be able to do it on a cheap or worthless piece of land. You're looking for a small island where the land is only connected to about ninety degrees of the island's circle. The land should be at least five acres.

You might have to get an environmental attorney to get the land approved for the use, but it's a low approval. The idea is to get about one hundred people paying $500 per month for a spot on this useless wetland island.

If you can put some kind of pole building or not, permit building on the land to create an office and/or boat repair building, you can probably pull in another $200,000 a year in boat repair business and maybe even new and used boat sales. You might have to put stones in for parking so the water flows through.

The income would be almost limitless because of your location. Picture an area that the land is priceless, and you can make a worthless piece of land valuable.

The potential is endless if you can get it approved. You might have to hire an engineer to get the approvals, but it's worth it. In this day and age where the waterfront property is slowly diminishing, especially in Florida where the price to keep a boat in the water has doubled in the last decade, it will be nice to know that you can still do something about it if you're able.

Well, for what's it worth, the answer is a small fortune you would have, one hundred floating homes in the water. Incidentally, one of these floating homes sells for $150,000 plus.

So the sales aspect is astronomical. The boat repair work demands about $80 per house and then you put a couple boat stackers on the land. Get yourself a forklift to drop the boats in front of the boat stacker; when the boat owner calls and says, "I'll be there at 2:00 p.m. to have my boat in the water," and then when he leaves you put it back on the boat stacker.

So let's see what we have. We got one hundred floating homes at $500 a month; that's $500,000 a year, plus your new floating home sales, plan the rental boats maybe another $150,000 a year, plus the repair work another $250,000 a year. Oh man, your worthless piece of land is netting you about $400,000 per year; a 10 percent income cap rate brings the value at about $4 million.

Chapter 25

How to Develop a Horse Stall Condominium Complex

YOU MUST FIND A piece of land that is out of the country, about one hundred acres. The land must be with access to major highways, so it's easy to get from a major city. Once you've found the land, contact the owner and ask him to sell it to you under the following terms and conditions, contingent upon getting zoning for a horse farm for one hundred horses.

You go into contract for one year to get approvals. The owner must give you the property for one year to get these approvals. During that approval process, you are going to get a group together to syndicate the operation, again with you as a general partner in a limited partnership. You might want to advertise your syndication to horse lovers, maybe in a horse magazine or a newspaper for horses.

You then line up your engineer, architect, accountant, and attorney, all working on a contingency. You might even give them a small piece of the partnership in lieu of getting paid.

The engineer will create a topographic study of the land to see where the location of your building will be. The stalls will be approximately five by ten feet with a corridor down the center to access your horse. You will also need a paddock to hold the horses in and land available for the horses to graze on.

Depending on what kind of horses you board, you might need a jumping ring or show ring. The farm should back up to some state-owned property so the tenants will have someplace to ride their horses.

To give you an idea of what the income and expense will be, it's going to cost you monthly mortgage payment, gas, electric, fixed and unfixed expenses. Have your accountant do an income and expense sheet so you can show to your investors what the bottom line will be.

The average rental should be in the area of $150 to $175 a month, plus feed, blankets, and medical expenses, say $20,000 per month; that's $250,000 a year, plus other fees such as exercising your horse, training your horse, and other expenses to be determined. You might also consider half a dozen or so horses to rent out for riding.

If you purchase horses of your own, the tax write-offs are great. You can write a live animal in eighteen months. Of course, the other write-offs mean depreciation on real estate, five years on equipment; you can pass write-offs on to your investors.

Chapter 26

How to Develop a Condo Hotel in a Resort Area

HOTEL CONDOMINIUMS GOT POPULAR in the eighties and went bananas. You find a hotel for sale in a resort area (I say a resort area because condos are second home for a lot of people) and the write-offs are astronomical. You approach the owner and put the hotel in contract, contingent upon getting it zoned as condominiums.

You again must tie the property up for a year to get the approvals. The cost for legal fees to convert a hotel into condos is about $30,000. Basically, what you're doing is converting rooms into fee simple residences. The idea is to pay approximately $30,000 per unit and sell them for $90,000 per unit; that's a gross profit of six million dollars—what a profit.

The hotel condos are the easiest thing to syndicate because of the profits and the great write-offs for those who purchase them. If a buyer pays $90,000 for a condo, it looks like this. The buyer gets thirty-one years' depreciation on the real estate; it becomes passive income if he allows the hotel to rent out his condo on a daily or weekly basis.

Passive income is like being in business: you get to write-off your condo fees, your property taxes, your vacancy factor, your utility bills, and the write-off is probably about $30,000 per year for a $90,000 investment.

When you form your syndication for investors, again you're going to be the general partner in a limited partnership. You want to advertise in the foreign newspaper first. To attract Chinese investors is good because the country took everything they had from them, so they want to leave. Africa did the same thing, so they want to leave also.

Again, you want to be able to buy your partners out after five years after they receive the five-year depreciation on furniture and fixtures, and there are a lot of furniture and fixtures in a hotel.

So at the end of five years, you will own the operating entity of the hotel and the condo association, worth about $3.75 million, free and clear.

You must do this deal with the anticipation of owning it, and do not let anyone talk you out of owning it.

After you convert the rooms into condos, you could even time-share them, but we'll go into time-sharing in another chapter.

Chapter 27

How to Syndicate a Feedlot

A FEEDLOT IS A way to raise cattle in a limited amount of space in your local area. The reason for feedlots is because when they move cattle across country, they tend to lose about forty lbs., plus you have the transportation cost. It tends to be a large expense as opposed to raising the cattle close by.

The feedback stalls are five feet by ten feet for each animal. They are separated by fences, and each animal has his own feeders and water supply. The feedback is under roof with climate-controlled buildings. It is good to have your feedlot close to a large city, where you can slaughter the animals and take the meat to market nearby.

You're going to need about ten acres of land in an agricultural area, with city water and sewerage, unless you put in your own recovery system for sewerage. You will build your feedlot; it can be a butler or pastel-steel building, about five thousand sq. ft., and you want to be able to accommodate three hundred to four hundred animals.

The animals, depending on what you feed them, will be strong and healthy cows with not a lot of muscle, but all the tender and meaty cows. The cows that are raised in hilly mountain-type areas are muscular because of the hills they walk up and down on, whereas your cows will make better eating, not tough-meat cows.

The syndication you put together must be with farm animal-type investors. You could advertise in the agricultural magazines or newspapers that are read by these types of individuals. Once again, your ad will read, "Syndication on large cow feedlot, investors needed. Great returns, minimum investment of $50,000. Please call."

Then set up your meetings with your investors as they call. Have information to show them at your meeting as to performers on how much money they can make and what the return on investment is. Remember, you can write-off an animal in eighteen months; you can get great write-offs with cows.

Then again, you put together your limited partnership with you as the general partner and get your engineer and architect to design your building and layout your land. And then you need your attorney to form your partnership and go to settlement for you and an accountant to do your performer, showing the income and expense sheet for your investors to see. Remember, your professional people will get paid double only after you put the syndication together with syndication money.

This is a huge moneymaking idea. Don't be afraid of it. It really works well, and you can make a lot of money putting a deal like this together. Remember to buy your partners out after five years, after they receive their five-year level depreciation on equipment.

Chapter 28

How to Syndicate a Foreign

Export-Import Business

THERE ARE SOME OVERSEAS products you can import that are very valuable and rare in our country. A friend of mine purchased an older 727 Boeing airplane from one of the airlines and decided to import some items that were rare in our country.

He kept the plane on the southern West Coast, so it would be easy to fly over the Fiji Islands. When landing his plane on the airfield over there, he could see natives paddling out in their canoes to dive for shellfish, which bore a strong resemblance to a lobster, that is, they had the big tails but smaller claws.

Each day, these natives would bring back a canoe full of these things. My friend thought what a great idea to open a small freezer plant over there and fly this lobster-like shellfish back to the States. He started to build his plant, and while the plant was under construction, he thought, *Well, there are a lot of other things that are rare in the United States that I could import.*

So my friend decided to build a small plant to make handbags out of iguana and snake skin. The Philippine mahogany was also in great demand to boat builders and furniture manufacturers. So he wound up building a sawmill along with other buildings.

Of course, when he first got the idea, he decided to get investors interested in his plan. So he formed a syndication by putting an ad in a Hong Kong newspaper to advertise his idea. The response was astronomical; he got so many calls he didn't know how to handle it. Because many of the countries over there were taking land and businesses away from their residents, they were glad to deal with a nation that was free country owned.

Today, my friend is one of the biggest importers in that region. So you see how an idea can come to fruition? Of course, my friend found other islands with rare items to import, and he became very friendly with the directors of the interiors in those islands. Because of the imports, he made had an impact on economic development and the trade unions, which afterward, he got involved with.

The guy was a policeman in the United States when he started, so to get himself started, he got a bunch of policemen to invest in the business. I remember he was a very nice man, easygoing, and fun to be around, which is very important when you're in business with someone. I also remember he was a very firm, strong businessman.

My friend now has several planes flying to several different locations and has become a billionaire in his own right. I recently heard he passed away, but I guess we all have to go when our time is up.

Chapter 29

How to Syndicate an Apartment Building and Make It into Condos or Co-Ops

You must find an apartment building that is for sale and you can purchase at a reasonable rate. You then approach the owner to sell you the property. You tell the owner exactly what you are trying to do so there are no surprises later on.

You tell the owner that you wish to put a group together to purchase his apartment building and that you're going to convert it into condominiums and sell them out to make a profit for your investors.

There is enough profit in this venture that you're not going to argue too much over price. The main thing you want to do is get control over the property. When you go into agreements on any property, you automatically have control over the property; as long as you do everything in that agreement, the seller can't get out of the deal.

So you don't have to purchase a real estate to control it. All you have to do is go into agreements on it. Once you get into agreements for 120 days, you can syndicate it, you can flip it, and you can do whatever you wish because you have the property tied up.

Your next stop once you get the property in agreements is to put an ad in a large city newspaper that you are looking to syndicate a condominium complex, which is an apartment conversion.

Advertise, saying, "Syndication condo complex, minimum investment of $50,000. Meeting on Wednesday at 8:00 p.m. at the Holiday Inn."

At this point, you should have everything together for your group to review the deal. The lawyer you hired on a contingency basis for double the fee, contingent upon being able to put the deal together and sell it out, already did your agreements, and you can start your condo conversion process. The accountant that you hired, also on a contingency basis, has already, at this point, done a projected performance as to the cost of the conversion and what the units will sell for when they're sold and so on.

It would also be good to have the contractor, who is going to do the work for you, at that meeting. The contractor gets paid out of the proceeds of the money you raise for the deal. He can give you the cost of conversion at the meeting.

As part of the deal, you'll probably need an engineer to get though the township for your condo conversion. Let's see now where we're at, say you purchase the apartment building for $30,000 per unit. If it's a regular residential nationhood, you should get about $90,000 per unit. If it's a seashore location, you would get between $125,000 and $175,000; of course, the cost of the apartments would be higher. Once again, you form your limited partnership with you as general partner. The deal becomes simpler as you go along. Again, make sure that you have the option to buy your partners out after they receive the five-year depreciation on equipment and fixtures. Use your profits to buy them out at that point. Then you will own 100 percent of the condo association after they are all sold out.

A co-op, on the other hand, is a corporation that owns the building. If it's one hundred apartments, each tenant tower owns 1 percent of the corporation. It's cheaper than doing a condo conversion, but they would sell for a lot less money.

Chapter 30

How to Syndicate a Condominium Shopping Center

FIRST, FIND A SHOPPING center for sale. Approach the owner and ask him how much he wants for his center. It would be better, at first, to have him hold a mortgage for five years. You tell the owner that you are going to syndicate the center to raise money to take the center out. You tell the owner that you want to convert the center over to condominiums and sell them out to make profit for your group. Owners seem to get excited when you mention syndication to them.

The owner must give you the center for a year so that you can go through your approval process. You do not argue about the price; there is enough profit in this deal that you do not have to do so. You approach an attorney first and try to get the attorney in on a contingency that when you convert the center and sell the units, you will pay him double his fee.

You have your attorney draw up the agreements of sale for the seller to sign. You then put him to work getting the township to agree to convert the shopping center into condominiums. Your story for the township is that it will raise the ratables and the taxes will go one and a half times what they are now.

It's now time to form your syndication; you put an ad in a large nearby city newspaper. "Syndication large shopping center conversion to condominiums, minimum investment of $50,000. Attend the meeting Tuesday night at the Ramada Inn at 7:30." At that meeting, you will have your attorney present. From now on, your attorney will handle a lot of things for you, but don't give him any power over the deal. If the investors are interested, you get a 10 percent deposit from them at the meeting; you will have your attorney put the money in an escrow account till final settlement.

The accountant that you are going to use will do a breakdown of cost to convert how much you're paying for the center, how much you will sell the stores to users for and so on. The accountant is also hired in a contingency basis and will get double when the deal settles and sells out.

The township may require an engineer to lay out the center and explain what you are doing. The engineer is also on a contingency basis and will get paid double at the end of the deal. You will pay approximately three million dollars for the center and sell it out for six million; it will make a three-million-dollar gross profit before expenses.

Once again, make sure that you can get the investors in the deal to sell out to you after they receive their five-year depreciation. Use your profit in the deal to buy them out for an agreed price. You'll wind up with a valuable condo association forever once the stores are sold out.

A co-op is a corporation that owns the center; if there are twenty stores, then each owner will pay his share of the rateables. The problem with co-op is that it won't be as profitable for you, but if for some reason you don't get the condo conversion, you might have to go that route. Instead of making three million, you'll only make two million or so. This book is only saying that you'll make a million a year with no money.

Chapter 31

How to Convert an Office Building into Condo Offices

You FIND AN OFFICE building for sale in a good area that's not all rented. You do the demographic studies to determine the area population in the surrounding area. The East Coast is a good area, between New York and Philadelphia in 150 miles by 150 miles, which area has a third of the population of the United States. You want an area with a million people in ten square miles and half a million people in five square miles, if possible.

You approach the owner in the usual manner, asking him how much he wants for this building. You tell him that you're going to syndicate it and convert it into condominiums. You tell him that if he gives you the place for a year, you can convert it into condos. So you go into the contract with him and start your syndication to raise the money to buy the building and convert it.

The highest and best use for the building would be a medical building. You would start by lining up different kinds of doctors, such as a chiropractor, a cardiologist, a dentist, and a urinary doctor, a foot doctor, an optician, and so on. The profit in converting and building to suit their needs is insatiable. You then hire an architect and an engineer to design the offices according to the wants and needs of these doctors.

You can probably purchase the offices for $50,000 per unit and sell them for $150,000 and $175,000 per unit, when fitted and finished. Another use would be a professional building with a lawyer, a CPA accounting firm, a real estate firm, an engineering firm, an architect, a place where you can walk in and put a whole deal together in one place. Once again, you're going to build to suit each individual.

Let's see now, you paid about $50,000 per unit, you put in another $20,000 per unit, that's $70,000, and you sell them for say $150,000 per unit. That's $80,000 profit multiplied by thirty units that totals approximately $2.4 million in profits. Not bad for a year's work.

You want to raise money to do the project, so you put an ad in the paper, saying, "Syndication office conversion into condominiums. Minimum investment of $50,000. Great writes-offs and depreciation. Meeting Wednesday night at 7:00 at the Holiday Inn."

At this point, you already hired an attorney, an architect, an engineer, and an accountant, all in a contingency basis. You offer to pay them all double, but they have to wait till you sell the project to get paid or maybe you would get them to invest in the project themselves. They would have to put up the $50,000 each upfront and get paid for their services on the back end.

You can make the same money in a year than some people make in a lifetime with my book; you just have to believe that you can do it.

Chapter 32

How to Convert a Warehouse into Condominiums

You find a large warehouse for sale in an area that's between other warehouses and residentially zoned area. You approach the owner and ask him how much he wants for his property.

He says, "I don't know what it's worth is to you."

You throw a number out at him, and he comes back and says no.

Then you say, "Well, I don't know how much to offer you, give me an idea."

When he comes back with a number, tell him you'll think about it. Remember, when you put the idea of selling into someone's head, they'll start talking to other people. You don't want them to get too many ideas, so you get back to them in a couple of days with your counteroffer.

You tell him that you are going to syndicate his property and that you are going to convert it to condominiums and sell them out individually to make money for your group. You tell him that you need to have the property for a year in order to convert it to condos because that's how long the process takes. You tell him that if you don't buy the property in a year, the money you will spend will make the property very valuable to him and that you will give him all of the approvals free of charge.

You go into agreements with the seller and start to form your syndication to raise money to purchase the property and convert it. You put an ad in a large city newspaper, where you will get a lot of activity or response to it. If you don't get the kind of response you want, go wider and deeper; advertise in the Hong Kong News, the Wall Street Journal, bigger newspapers with more distribution. Once again you hire your accountant, your engineer, your attorney all on a contingency basis. You offer to pay them double if they wait till you sell the project.

Then you have your attorney draw up the papers. The wording you will use will be your name or nominee or assignee, New Jersey if you're in New Jersey, the corporation to be formed, hereafter known as buyer.

This gives many options on what to do with the property once you get it into agreements. Remember, you don't have to buy a property to do anything with it; you merely have to put it in agreements to control it. As long as you do everything that the agreement says, you can do whatever you want with the property and the owner can't get out of the deal.

You then will advertise syndication, saying, "Fifty thousand dollars' minimum investment on warehouse conversion to condominiums. Meeting at the Ramada Inn, Tuesday night at 7:00."

At this point, you should have your people around you to help you close the deal; the more people at your meeting, the better. Remember, a trip of a thousand miles starts with the first step. Remember that in order to do this deal, you must move forward with unwavering courage and mastery of detail.

Now, let's say you buy the warehouse for $500,000, and it's 75,000 sq. ft. You take 20 percent for excess and egress; that's 80 percent for usage and that's sixty thousand sq. ft. to be used. Using one thousand sq. ft. units at $110,000 a unit times sixty equals $6.6 million conversion cost, about $25,000 per unit, that leaves almost five million in profits. Wow!

Make sure you get your professional people together and set up your meeting with your investors; make sure everyone you're paying does their part. Have the engineer explain how the place is going to be laid out, with pictures from the architect. Have the accountant break down how much each partner will get out of the deal and when. Also, have the accountant get everyone a breakdown of what writes-offs each owner/member will get; that's very important to those who make several hundred thousand a year in your group. They could possibly get their investment back in two years in tax breaks, plus whatever they make on the deal.

Remember, you're paying these people double for their work because they're doing it on a contingency basis. The best place, if you can get it, is a waterfront property. Many areas are converting their once waterfront industrial site into condos and single-family houses detached and semi-detached.

If you can get in before the developers and convert your warehouse into loft apartments, you have a home run. Waterfront loft apartments draw a nicer income than non-waterfront units. If you have Riparian rights and you have a boat slip with each unit, you can draw an even higher amount when selling out the units. Remember, if you get into an area which is marked for waterfront development, once you get the approach and build, you will be grandfathered in to your conversion.

This was the Executive Inn Banquets, 750 seats in Vineland owned by Bob Domico and Grace Baldwin. It is presently the Ramada Inn.

Chapter 33

How to Convert a Warehouse into a Ministorage Facility

FIND A WAREHOUSE FOR sale on a busy highway with a lot of visibility. Approach the owner and tell him you would like to purchase his warehouse for your company to convert to another use. Do not tell him what you are going to do with the building; it's too easy for him to convert it himself once you gave him the idea.

You must move quickly on this deal because it's a very good deal, and if you don't get it into agreement right away, you'll lose it. You try to get it into agreements as fast as you can. Tell the owner that you would like a six-month settlement date because you have a 1031 real estate exchange and that you have to wait six months to close.

Hurry and put your syndication together by putting your ad in the paper: "Syndication warehouse conversion into mini-warehouse; $50,000 minimum of investment—hurry, won't last. Meeting Thursday night at Holiday Inn at 7:00." You laid out the plan to your investors; keep the investors away from the property until you definitely have the property tied up with the owner.

What you're going to do is hire a company to build a wire-type fence inside your warehouse, separating the units from one another. Compared to what you're paying per square foot; the profits are humongous. You will be renting out your space for approximately

$18 a foot per year; your cost to convert to mini-warehouse is $3 per foot.

The owner that sold you the property will be upset when he finds out what you want to do with the property. So get him tied up as soon as you can and make sure he is locked into the deal. If he finds out what you're doing, he will try to keep you from getting the small zoning change that you need.

Try to find at least a hundred thousand sq. ft. warehouse with parking for about twenty cars. You can fill up your warehouse by buying a diesel truck and picking up the items for storage with no charge. Once their items are in, they have to pay you; otherwise, you will auction off their items.

How much money will you make? An obscene amount. You're probably going to buy the warehouse for $10,000 per square foot and take off 20 percent for hallways and turnarounds. You'll probably spend about $3 per foot to convert the use and $2 per foot for miscellaneous, say $5 per foot and you're going to get $18 per foot per year rent. I'm not even going to run the numbers for you, you do it yourself.

You'll find that this is one of the high-end profit ventures you'll get involved with in your life. So move forward on this deal ASAP. There are many deals that make money as you read through these pages. You must get started if you want to hit it big.

Chapter 34

How to Convince Lawyers, Accountants, Engineers, and Architects They Should Work for You on a Contingency Basis

When you approach a professional person to work for you on a contingency basis, the first thing they are going to say is "I can't do it, I don't have the time" or "I can't afford to put my time into something that is not immediately fruitful to me." Convince them that you're paying them double and it would be like doing two jobs instead of one.

First, you're going to approach someone maybe that is just starting out or someone who has experience but it's his slow time of the year or maybe his office is not that busy right now. Remember, you're working with no money, and in order to put this deal together, you must get these people to work on a contingency basis.

If the person is just starting out, you have to convince them that it's an opportunity for them to get in on the ground floor with you, and that if you're successful in your endeavors, they will be able to go all the way with you. After all, if you're able to pull this deal off, you will be a very wealthy person, and on the next deal, you'll be able to pay them upfront.

You'll be able to do many deals after that because they will gain experience in your type of deal and be able to know what is coming down on the road on the next deal.

Even if you approach a more experienced person, they're liable not to be experienced in the job that they will do for you. I recently put an ad on the Internet for sale certificates, and three lawyers called and asked me if I wanted them to represent me with their clients in selling the tax sale certificates that they could help me sell them, and they had a lot of clients that would like to purchase them.

So you see there's a lot of hungry lawyers out there looking for something more to do with their time. The other thing you could do is to maybe offer them a small piece of the deal upfront, if it is successful. After all, you'll be able to afford them afterward, and because they helped you from the beginning, you would trust them more and keep them with you for the next deal.

Convince them that you're going to make a lot of money because you're a person that goes all the way and doesn't quit. You could offer them, say, 5 percent ownership in the entire deal with an option to buy them at the end. I can assure that they've never seen a deal like what you're trying to put together, so maybe it would be exciting to go along with you and see where the deal goes. It would be hard for them to turn you down, and your deal happens to be successful.

Remember, you need these people to succeed, and it would be difficult without their help and expertise. You'll gain more experience from using the expertise of others. Another thing you could do is offer them a small token when you begin to first put the deal together out of the investment money that you collected in the beginning; of course, let the investors know that part of their money is going to be used for professional people to assist you with your approvals and so on.

In any case, don't give up. Remember, you need these people to go through the approval process. You may have to approach many professional people to be able to go forward with a deal. When you approach the people, be nice and sincere. Don't act like you know it all. Be humble, but not to the extent of being not knowledgeable.

Chapter 35

How to Put Together a Fleet of Charter Boats for Lease or to Syndicate and Sell Them Out to Fifty Owners Per Boat One Per Week Each Ownership to Time-Share

A FRIEND OF MINE called me about five years ago and told me he was buying a fifty-four-foot sailboat out of Hurricane Katrina. The boat was destroyed, but he wanted to restore the boat, bring it back to its original condition, and charter it out for cruises. I wasn't interested at the time, but he called a year later and told me the boat was finished and if I wanted to sail over to the Bahamas with the boat. The boat had three bedrooms and three baths, so we could do it with three couples.

The boat was in Daytona Beach, Florida, so it was only a day's cruise over there, and so I decided to go. We got underway, and it was the most beautiful experience I think I have ever had. The cruise was like a dream. I don't know if you've ever been sailing, but standing in the back of the boat steering it, it's like the wind is in the back of you, pushing this very large sailboat across the water in a pristine fashion.

We moored out of Grand Bahamas and took the little dingy into the shore. It was like you were in Monte Carlo or someplace going into the casino for the day, wonderful. We spent a week there and had a wonderful time. I decided afterward that I liked this life and maybe I want to be involved in this life a little. I was older now and this is so relaxing. At night, we would stay on the boat. In the morning, we would swim in the clear water, spear fish, or just bask in the sun all day with a cool drink. We started a charter business out of Daytona Beach. I went into partners with my friend.

We had day trips. We had many trips to a lot of different places that I had never been before, for a week at a time.

One day, I said to my partners, "Why don't we do a syndication to purchase some more boats and maybe time-share them or give fifty people a week each and let them own a boat like ours?"

We purchased another large boat, fixed it up, and did a time-share with it with fifty people. Each person would take the boat for a week, with several couples, and either we would go with them, if they didn't know how to sail, or they would take the boat themselves if they had a captain's license.

We paid $55,000 for the wrecked boat. We had to replace the masts, the motor, the sails, the, generator; everything was either ruined or stolen from the wrack. It cost us about another $50,000 to fix up the boat, but when we got finished, it was worth $250,000. So we sold the fifty weeks of time-share for $10,000 per week or $500,000.

Time-shares are interesting to people who don't want to spend $300,000 for a boat because they don't use it that much. If you use a boat a month out of the year, you buy four weeks for forty thousand rather than spending $300,000 for the boat. With that time-share, we included slip fees and insurance, so you get a boat for as much as a year as you use it. Plus, the tax write-offs are great. If income bracket is great, it would cost you hardly anything at all.

That was five years ago; we've done the same thing several times over and made a very successful business out of this idea. Just another idea for you, and remember, you can always syndicate this deal if you don't have the money to do it yourself. That's the whole idea of my book, deals like this that make a lot of money, with no money.

Chapter 36

Owning Land under Very Valuable Property Is Definitely a Way to Create Great Wealth

IN 1970, I WAS with a friend of mine who purchased a piece of land in Atlantic City. The land was a two hundred feet by four hundred feet corner property. The idea was that gambling was soon going to come to Atlantic City.

My friend waited for two years after that, and gambling came forward on the referendum, but it was turned down. So he decided to sell the boardwalk side of my land, actually one-half of my land, which was two hundred feet by two hundred feet. Actually, it was the oceanfront part of my land; he sold it to a recreational developer who was planning to build a casino on the site once gambling was approved. So at the time, I thought it happened to be a casino using a concealed name.

My friend paid $75,000 for the whole piece, so he thought the land was a good deal to sell half of the land for $175,000 at the time, so he sold it. He still owned the land between where he sold and the front street. The gambling came back up on the referendum and was voted in. My friend was approached again by the casino to sell the other piece, but now he knew that they were going to build a casino on it, so he refused to sell it.

He drew up a twenty-year lease for the land, which I still owned for $75,000 a year for twenty years. The lease expired in 1991, so he renewed the lease with the casino, this time for $150,000 a year for ten years. The lease expired again in 2001. He renewed the lease again with the casino for ten years, and this time, he asked $200,000 per year and got it. When the lease expires again in 2011, he will ask $300,000 a year for the rent.

Using a 10 percent capitalization rate in 2011, the property will be worth $3 million—not bad for a $75,000 investment. You can purchase land for a song before development comes in, but again, land with no income is very hard to hold on to.

You must have a plan on what you're going to do with it. My friend almost lost the land back to the bank because he had a bad year in 1973 when the economy was bad. McDonald's was up 25 percent because everybody was eating hamburgers. And all the large eat-in restaurants were closing up, right and left.

Marriott Corporation converted all their small cafeterias to Hot Shoppes, and they started a new restaurant called Phineas Prime and another chain called Josiah Tree and several other steakhouse franchise that were only open at dinnertime. Then they opened the Roy Rodgers chain.

The year 1973 was a bad year; there was a terrific gas shortage and the cars were lined up at the gas pumps in droves. I remember I purchased a 240 D Mercedes Benz, which was a diesel, a four-cylinder engine, which got thirty-five miles to the gallon and then I put another gas tank in it. So I was able to travel 720 miles without stopping for fuel.

After gambling came to Atlantic City, my friend purchased useless pieces of wetlands to put billboards in coming Atlantic City, which he was able to get variance on. To put billboards on entering Atlantic City, which he still owns, yields a very good return also.

In 1974, another friend and I purchased a large restaurant across the street from Marina district. The restaurant had a motel in the back of it, so we did a ten-year lease purchase for $2,500 a month for ten years; the rent was to come off the purchase price, which was $600,000. It was an 850-seat restaurant, which was also built in expectations of gambling coming in.

The area coming in was to be for roulette tables and chap tables, and the other rooms were for blackjack and other games such as slot machines and so on. In those days, nobody knew that you had to have five hundred rooms and a minimum 25,000 sq. ft. of gambling area to build a casino. Everybody thought they would come in with the mom-and-pop operations like they had in Las Vegas. The guy that built the restaurant would open as a restaurant and then convert it over to a gambling hall afterward. The guy that built the restaurant was older, and he had a heart attack six months after he opened it.

So my friend bought the place on a lease-purchase arrangement. After we were opened for a year, a large hotel owner decided to build a casino on the site that we had purchased. They started syndication much like the ones in my book. One of the guys in the syndication was an attorney, who in the old days represented Al Capone, the Chicago gangster. The hotel that was built was turned down by the gambling commission for a gambling license.

So the hotel owner said, "I'll never build another hotel in New Jersey for the rest of my life," but he did anyway.

Well, so the story goes. The hotel owner had built this beautiful five-hundred-room casino and spent three hundred million doing it and couldn't get a license. Another casino owner came along and offered the guy that built the hotel $25 million more for the property than it cost him to build.

At the time, my friend owned about 35 percent of the land under the casino, if he exercised my option for the restaurant and motel land underneath. So the windup was after he did that, he owned about 35 percent of the land under the casino.

He drew up a lease for the land under the casino for twenty years for $350,000 per year. This lease expired in 1994, and we renewed it for $450,000 a year for another ten years, which expired in 2004, and which we renewed again for another ten years for $550,000 a year. Using a 10 percent capitalizing rate, according to the present income, the land is worth $5.5 million, not bad for a $650,000 investment. So you see it's not hard to become very wealthy; you just have to be in the right place at the right time.

Chapter 37

Monologue of a Salesman

How GOOD OF A salesman are you? How far would you go to make one million or five million dollars? In order to be a good salesman, you must first qualify your customers. Make sure that there is no doubt in your mind that the person you are trying to sell something is qualified to buy it. As long as the person has the money or the means to get the money to buy what you want to sell, then I'll teach you how to sell it to her or him.

You must investigate your potential investors, check them out, make sure they have the wherewithal to purchase part of the deal you're selling. It's a big waste of time to try to sell something to someone that would like to purchase what you're selling, but he just can't; even if he is a nice guy that you would like to have in your group, he just can't qualify.

First, you must advertise whatever it is you're selling in the right place. Large city newspapers which wealthy people read; little papers in small towns never have the exposure that these large newspapers have. If it's a big enough deal, use the New York Times, the Wall Street Journal, and the Hong Kong News.

You want the wealthiest people, so you use the biggest and best newspapers. Don't be afraid to talk to these people. You're selling the best deals in the world; sell your heart out. The more confident you feel, the better you'll sell to this person. Remember that you don't have any money and you're trying to use other people's money, so you have to sell just a little bit harder than normal. The product that you're selling is the highest and best product you can sell; you just have to believe in it before you can sell it to someone else.

Once you believe in what you're selling, it will become easier for you. You must back up everything you're selling with research. Study the product, and make it the best deal in the world. Tell the investor about the profits that he can expect; tell him about the tax write-offs he will receive. Make him see that he can't get hurt in the deal and to help you convince others in the syndication that it's a good deal as well.

Once you get a couple of professionals involved in your deal, the driving urge will make you succeed. Make sure before you meet with your potential investors that you have all the figures from the accountant, the engineering reports, the architectural drawings, and all your legal planning in line.

Some people with money tend to treat you like you're a second-class citizen. Discard that person and go to the next one. Some people have more compassion than others and are much easier to talk to. There are millions of people that you can talk about your deal. Don't dwell on certain people who would give you a hard time. After all, it's your deal, and it's yours to sell and keep.

Chapter 38

How to Syndicate Condominium Boat Slips

BACK IN THE LATE '70s, I forgot the year, I was invited to a large condominium slip sale in a marina that was going bankrupt. This marina was built by the largest distributor of boat bulge pumps. The slips were going for three and four thousand dollars a slip.

I purchased five slips at the sale, and now they are worth $1,000 per foot, forty foot slips for forty thousand dollars. The rent on the slips is between $4,000 and $5,000 per slip per summer season.

You can get another $1,500 a year if they decide to leave their boat in for the winter. The marina runs everything, which is fine with me; I gladly pay them their 10 percent fee for renting the slips out for me each year. It's good to use the marina to rent out your slips for you, just to have them on your side if something bad happens. Like a big northeastern storm, or a hurricane, or any other catastrophic emergency, or someone bumping into one of your rental boat slips.

When the marina builder decided to go into bankruptcy, he bankrupted the corporation and held on to the condominium association, wherein he collects approximately $2,000 condo fees for each slip, which wasn't a bad deal for him. If you ever get in that situation, you'll know what to do.

Well, that's where I got the idea to buy the marinas and convert them into condominium slips. I went to the Chesapeake Bay to look for marinas for sale; they seem to be the popular place to keep your boat located between Washington, DC, and Philadelphia. It seemed to be a haven for boats forty-foot plus, where you could make a nice profit doing a condo conversion and selling forty-plus slips.

The marinas at the time, when I went into it, were selling for about an average of about $12,000 per slip. The cost to convert them, besides the legal fees, was about $4,000 per slip.

So by time you purchased them, converted them, and sold them out, it cost you $12,000 to purchase them, $4,000 a slip to put in floating docks. You had to build a seawall outside of the marina to prevent waves from coming in from the intercoastal and rocking the boats. Plus, your legal fees for your condo conversion, it's going to cost you about $20,000 per slip, and they would sell for an average of $40,000 per slip and that's if you sold them yourself and didn't pay any broker's fees.

So let's see now, an average marina of three hundred slips would sell for $3.6 million and you would sell it out for approximately $7.2 million after expenses at a profit of about $3.6 million. Not a bad day's work, as they say.

You have to purchase the marina first, get it in contract for at least a year because you have to convert it, and of course, you're going to tell the seller that if you are not able to convert it, you will deliver to him all the approvals that you received if you don't purchase the marina at the end.

Once you get it in contract, you'll want to start your syndication. First, put an ad in a large newspaper in a large nearby city, saying, "Syndication on marina condo conversion, minimum investment of $50,000."

Hire your new aquatic engineer to design your new marina. Have the drawings finished before you start the syndication. Your engineer is hired on a contingency basis, your lawyer who is going to do your conversion package and your agreements of sale and so on is hired on a contingency basis, and your accountant is also hired the same way. Remember, you don't have any money to do this deal on your own, so you have to pay these professional people double at the end.

Remember that the people you bring in to the syndication are high earners and need tax write-offs. When you acquire a marina, the personal property is a big part of the tax deduction. Equipment and fixtures, namely the piers and docks, are quickly deducted with fast depreciation were the real estate, which is the smaller part of the tax breaks are deducted over a longer period. This type of real estate transaction provides an excellent tax shelter investment.

Chapter 39

How to Get Very Wealthy on Residential Real Estate Starting with Your Residence

STARTING WITH THE EQUITY in your house, you can gain much wealth. You must first go out and mortgage your house to the hilt.

You then look for great real estate deals that are hard to find, such as people losing their house with a lot of equity in it.

You approach these people and give them a couple of thousand dollars and they sign over a quitclaim deed and leave the premises. You may go to a sheriff's sale and someone buys a great house for a low price, then you go to the owner of the house and offer him a couple of thousand dollars to hand over the quitclaim deed to you. He has ten days to redeem it from the sheriff and pay back the guy the money that he paid for it at the sheriff's sale. You then go and redeem the house, then you own it.

The next thing you will do is to go out and take a mortgage out on the new house you just bought. Say for instance, that the house was worth $200,000 and you bought it for $80,000, you can borrow 80 percent loan to value. So now you borrow 80 percent of $160,000. If you paid $80,000 for the house, then you get to put $80,000 in your pocket. Then you will rent the house out, and the tenant will pay your mortgage off for you. Now you go back and pay off the money you borrowed on your house, as soon as you can. You should be able to do the next deal for cash. When you finance the next deal, you use the money to purchase another house and so on. In a normal market, the real estate will appreciate 12 percent a year, and if you buy a $200,000 home, it will go up $24,000 per year. If you have ten houses, your appreciation is $240,000 per year. It will take you a couple of years to get in that financial situation, but what else were you going to do in that couple of years.

Look at it this way, if you purchase a $200,000 home and you put down 10 percent, and it goes up 12 percent the first year you made $4,000 that year, the next year you'll make $12,000 from that house. As long as you rent the house out for enough to cover the expenses, then you have a win-win situation.

If you are buying an existing house from someone, you can make deals with discounts from the mortgages. The first mortgages, you can get from 10 percent to 40 percent, discounted off it, especially if the mortgage rate went up that year. You can discount the second mortgage because there is less chance the second mortgage will get paid off if someone were to foreclose on the property, and you can discount a second mortgage from 40 to 70 percent.

You should have a plan if you mortgage your house as to exactly what you're going to do and in how much time.

Remember, whenever you borrow money, you have to pay it back, and the law of diminishing returns will eat you up if you do not move quickly. If you get into a situation when you're not able to rent a house because of a problem with the township about not being able to get a certificate of occupancy or many other reasons, remember, you can always rent section 8 or you could always sell the house.

If you want to sell the house quickly, put it on multiple listings, and offer the selling real estate agent a $2,500 cash bonus a settlement. Make sure it's advertised on multiple listings that you're paying this extra money, and it would be advisable to send fliers out to all the local real estate companies that you're paying extra money to the selling agent. This way, every agent in the country will bring his or her clients to your house to get this extra money from you.

Remember, it's a matter of life and death to sell when you have to sell and buy when you have to buy.

Chapter 40

How to Use Your Commissions from Your Business Brokerage or Real Estate Company to Make Bigger and Better Deals

THE BEST AND EASIEST way to list and sell a business or piece of real estate, if you're a licensed real estate broker, is to put your commission back into the deal.

If you're not licensed to sell real estate, you can be a business broker. In most states, you don't need a license; you just need to register your business brokerage with the city and get a business permit.

If you're selling a motel to a group, for example, and they don't have the down payment, you can put up your commission for their down payment. It's going to make the deal fly, first of all, and you can collect a healthy money payment with interest for the next five years.

First of all, the advantage in being a business broker rather than a real estate broker is that you can charge less commission because of the fact that you're not a real estate broker. This means you can't charge a commission for selling real estate, and it doesn't mean you can sell real estate, it just means you don't get paid a commission for it.

For example, let's say you're selling a large restaurant for three million dollars. The restaurant business is worth $1.5 million and the real estate is worth $1.5 million. As a business broker, you are only going to charge for the business you're selling and not the real estate. So you're only charging 10 percent of $1.5 million or $150,000 instead of $300,000 dollars, like a real estate broker would charge. So who is the guy going to list with? The guy that charges $300,000 or the guy that charges $150,000?

So now you get the listing. How are you going to sell this large restaurant? Well, the first thing you are going to do is call all of the large restaurant chains and try to put a deal together with them; after all, they are taking less of a chance because it's already a restaurant. You do the demographics and the area input studies, then package it and send it to twelve or fifteen national restaurant companies.

Then if that doesn't work, you can always syndicate it and that's easy. Everyone wants to own part of a large restaurant where they can take their friends for dinner. If they're high-paying professional people, they can get great write-offs. A three-million-dollar restaurant has a million dollar-worth of equipment that can be written-off in five years. That's $200,000 a year write-off. Not bad, you split that up among five guys, that's a $40,000 a year for each partner.

Here's how to sweeten the deal: you're going to put your $150,000 commission back into the deal for the down payment. Now watch the deal really fly. So if you walk away, you'll have about $2,500 a month for five years.

Chapter 41

My First Syndication: Lucien's Old Tavern

IN 1982, I WAS partners in the real estate business with another fellow in Haddonfield. We had an office on the main drag. My partner got a telephone listing on an old tavern that was established in 1907 and was a stagecoach stop in older times halfway between Philadelphia and Atlantic City. The name of the place was Lucien's Old Tavern. It was an 850-seat restaurant, lounge, and banquet facility located in Berlin, New Jersey.

I decided to do my first syndication on that restaurant. Not like now where I would put an ad in the newspaper to advertise for investors, I decided to put this group together with people that I knew. I carefully selected two gentlemen who were experienced in the food and beverage business and one who was a developer, an architect, two accountants, and of course, my real estate partner and me. There were 5 to 20 percent shares put up, and my partner and I had 20 percent together.

The two food-and-beverage guys were to run the restaurant and everybody else had various jobs to do. It was a general partnership, where everyone was responsible for everything. We purchased the place on Saint Patrick's Day 1982, but on Memorial Day, the place burnt to the ground. The fire inspector said it was an electrical problem.

We decided to collect the insurance money and rebuild the place. Both of the restaurant guys wanted out, and my real estate agent partner wanted out after the fire. So we gave them back what they put into the deal and they left. We started construction and rebuilt the place and opened at the end of 1983. We opened up doing very well, and all the customers were glad to see the place opened up again. The two accountants, who now had 60 percent ownership in the restaurant at this point, took charge of the restaurant. The group still only approve them for $500 per month for their accounting. No one got any salaries.

In the beginning of 1985 after we did $2.7 million in business that year, the place started to make a few bucks. I put in three bridal shows a year and sent out 2,500 early warning Christmas party letters, and we booked about twenty weddings a year and had forty-seven groups to meet there once a month.

I decided to take everybody out and take over the place myself. I paid my partners with a seventy-thousand-dollar mortgage, which I got from a previous motel deal that I received for commission. I took out the a la carte service and made it a total banquet facility. The place that I set up went on to do five million a year. The new owners expanded the place from 17,000 sq. ft. to over 30,000 sq. ft. The place turned out to be a beautiful banquet facility, one of the nicest in the state.

This is Lucien's Old Tavern. Established in 1909, it was a stagecoach stop between Philadelphia and Atlantic City. This was Bob Domico's first large syndication. It was purchased on St. Patrick's Day, but then on Memorial Day, it burnt to the ground. It was rebuilt brand-new by Bob Domico and his partners and reopened again. Bob bought his partners out and took it over himself. It is presently Lucien's Manor in Berlin, New Jersey.

Steppin' Out Restaurant of the Week

by Harry Swiderski

Waiter Jimmy Stillwell pours coffee for long-time patrons Mr. and Mrs. G. Leonard Heck Jr. of Haddonfield.

What started out as a stagecoach stop between Philadelphia and communities in South Jersey in 1781 is now one of the areas finest restaurants—Lucien's, located at 81 White Horse Pike in Berlin, N.J.

Owner Bob Domico has assembled a staff that is dedicated to providing the utmost in dining pleasure. The restaurant severely damaged by a May 1982 fire has been completely renovated and presents an aura of stateliness.

The beautiful, long, white building offers a pleasant invitation to go in and dine. Once inside, the tasteful decor promises even more fine dining. Rose-colored drapes, colorful still-life paintings and tapestry covered chairs enhance the room.

It is soon apparent that repeat customers are plentiful and well-known to the experienced staff of waiters, some of whom have been employed at Lucien's for more than 25 years.

Pianist John Dale "serves" dinner music Monday through Thursday.

Up to 840 diners may be accommodated on both levels of the restaurant. Lucien's specializes in weddings and banquets of all sizes. The regular dining rooms will seat about 250 for a la carte menu selections.

Sunday brunch, a real bargain at $7.95, is extremely popular with Lucien's repeat patrons, and rapidly gaining a larger following. It is served from 11:00 a.m. to 2:00 p.m. Several daily luncheon specialties are added to the menu and an early bird offer includes full-course dining from 3:30 to 6:30 p.m. at $7.95.

Bob Domico, owner of Lucien's

Wednesday night is lobster night at $11.95. Thursday features prime ribs at $9.95. Friday it's Chipino for two at $19.95 per couple, and Sunday is duck night at $9.95.

Tuesday is couples' night and Lucien's provides four specialty items accompanied by a free 1/2 carafe of wine at $19.95 per couple. The special pork and sauerkraut served Tuesdays has been a Lucien's tradition for longer than anyone can remember.

Our visit was a delightful experience in fine dining. Everything was perfect, especially the visit with Domico, who is extremely proud of the 204-year history of the tavern.

We started our delicious meal with a really jumbo shrimp cocktail and a mountain of fresh melon for appetizers. This was followed by lobster bisque and baked French onion soups, the portions of which were large and very flavorful.

You salad lovers will have a real treat if you order Lucien's spinach salad as it is a picture of fine cuisine with its hard-boiled eggs, mushrooms, and bacon, doused with creamy hot dressing.

Our entrees were broiled, tender, and sweet lamb chops and a lobster and shrimp special, stir fried in a wine sauce that would enhance any main dish. Amaretto cake and orange and lemon sherbet satisfied the sweet tooth.

Diners are also treated to the piano playing of John Dale, Monday thru Thursday. Tony Stumpo draws large crowds with his special style on weekends.

For more information or reservations, call (609) 767-2500.

Hostess Joann Cathcart (L) and hostess Carole Abrams greet arrivals at Lucien's.

Chapter 42

Schrul's Restaurant: My Second Syndication

DURING THE TIME THAT Lucien's was open, I decided to do syndication. I put the word out to my friends and clients that I was doing syndication and decided to buy another landmark restaurant, one that was around seventy-five years old or so. The restaurant was located down the shore area in Egg Harbor Township, near Atlantic City.

I got five partners involved in this once, a widow, a local businessman, another realtor, an investor, and myself. Once again, in those days, a general partnership looked like the way to go. We put up $40,000 each, and the sale price was $675,000, which wasn't a bad price for a place that was doing $1.2 million a year.

We operated the place for a couple of years, and the widow and I bought everybody else out, then we sold it for $50,000 more than we paid for it. Now the area turned into the best area down the shore; the real estate values skyrocketed. You never know when you're going to make money quickly out of a deal or if you're going to make money or not.

My plan with Schrul's was to take the property and build an econo-lodge motel alongside it to create a good cash flow business. There was a great need for the offshore area of Atlantic City to have motels for the casino overflows, but the group I had didn't want to put any more money into the deal. It's very important to plan a whole scenario when you do a deal as to what you're going to do to expand the property and to increase its value. You have to have a plan to expand something, to make it more valuable or it's not worth pursuing a lot of times.

Such as converting an apartment building into condos or adding a specific performer to a project and producing the maximum usage out of it by creating its highest and best use. The restaurant went on to become a large high-end steakhouse. Today, it's a multimillion-dollar attraction. If we would have put the motel there, it would have been worth about six million today.

Today, if I put a group together, I would check out their financial ability to completely finish a project once the plan is set forth. You have to understand when I put Schrul's together, I wasn't that experienced in syndicating, but today I am. So today, I would plan the syndication with more intensity.

Remember, a restaurant deal is easy to put together because everybody, and their brother, wants to own a restaurant. You can take your friends to dinner in a restaurant that you're part owner of and the write-offs are phenomenal if you have other income.

I have had at least eleven restaurants in my life and have enjoyed owning every one of them. It's an easy syndication to put together and it really works well for you because of the advantages of owning a restaurant.

This is Schrul's Restaurant, which was established in 1907. It is owned by Bob Domico and Grace Baldwin, a 250-seat restaurant and lounge. It is presently the Berkshire Restaurant and Lounge in McKee City, New Jersey.

Chapter 43

My Third Syndication: Executive Banquets

My third syndication was a holiday inn in Vineland, New Jersey. The hotel was purchased by an Indian guy who had very little restaurant or banquet experience. We decided on a monthly rent; I don't remember exactly what it was now, but we opened up. It was a 750-seat facility with a small restaurant and coffee shop.

We went in immediately with a grand opening and then booked our first bridal show, which was very successful, except for the union coming in, demanding that all our employees join the union. I had never had any union in any of my places and didn't want any, so we fought them off. We started booking weddings right away and contacted all the local corporations for dinner meetings, conventions, Christmas parties, etc.

I remember starting a teen dance on Sunday nights. We called it War of the DJs, and every week, we would have a different high school represented to spin the records for the night; the windup was we built it up to 850 kids on a Sunday night at $5 per head.

It cost me $250 a night for a DJ and $35 each for two uniformed security guards, a door man, and a couple of bartenders that mixed drinks like piña colada and Harvey Wallbangers, neither of which had any booze in them. I remember I never made more money in that three-hour Sunday night dance in my life.

We begin booking bar mitzvahs, rehearsal dinners, bachelor's parties, promotions, bowling banquets, sweet sixteens—you name it, we booked it. The widow that I brought into Schrul's with me ran the show and did a great job.

I was very busy in those days with Lucien's, Schrul's, and Executive Banquets, as it was called. I began syndicating restaurants because of my father being in the restaurant business and banquet business and because of my extensive experience in a Green Valley Country Club and Dulles International Airport.

I figured if we did a million a year in banquets with a twenty gratuity, that would be $200,000 a year slam dunk. It was a nice easy business for us in those days. Eventually, we sold the place for a huge profit, and to think it didn't cost us a lot to get into it.

Actually, I did thirteen syndications in ten years. In those days, it took up a lot of my time. No use in talking about all of them. The whole idea is to put these things together, one after another, with not a lot of effort on your part; once you do a couple, it becomes easy. So get your first one started and start making money as fast as you want to do.

The book I'm writing is for the sole purpose of you making money from its content. It's a chance to do something big without putting any of your own money in.

Chapter 44

How to Put Syndication Together with Mirrors

Remember, you have no money, so you have to put this syndication together with mirrors. You first get on the phone and start calling large investment groups. Talk to doctors, lawyers, and Indian chefs that are in the high-income bracket that need write-offs. The more you talk, the better you sound. Polish your spiel, practice over and over what you are going to say, improve on your speech so you sound like you know what you're talking about, and do the research on the subject until you get it right.

By "mirrors," we mean that you're talking to the investors and at the same time you're talking to the sellers. You would have talked to a couple of dozen investors, so maybe you'll spark some interest. If so, ask the person that is interested if you can drop his name to the seller.

Don't give the investor too much information that he gets the idea he can go behind your back and put his own syndication together with his friends. You will go to the seller and let him know that you have plenty of investors to syndicate his property with. If it's a shopping center, let him know that you intend to "condominiumize" his property into separate units to make money for your investors. Maybe you could even ask the seller, after you get a couple of guys interested, if he would like to stay in as part owner of the syndication. Maybe the owner is tired of running the center himself, but maybe he doesn't want to get all the way out. You must be persistent with your ideas and keep the ball rolling, so to speak. Be able to move forward with unwavering courage and mastery of detail.

The same thing goes when you approach the lawyer who is going to represent you in this deal, the architect that's going to draw the plans to convert your project into condos, the engineer who is going to get you through the township so you can convert, and the accountant who is going to put the numbers together so you can convince the investors how good this deal is and how much money it will make for them and how many tax write-offs it will bring.

Remember, if an investor is already making a couple of hundred thousand a year, then he is paying about 28 percent of what he is making to the government, so he needs a write-off. You have to convince him to put $50,000 with you, rather than to throw it away to the government. If it's a large restaurant you're selling, then he can bring his friends in to eat at his own restaurant. If it's a mini-warehouse you're putting together, then he can offer his friends a discount to store their belongings in your own warehouse. It makes him feel generous, good, and friendly to his friends. Make sure if you invite the seller of the property into the investment that you already have it in agreements so that he doesn't get the idea he can syndicate the place himself without you. You must stay on top of these things to make them work, and remember, never, never, never give up. Some people will think you are a thief when they find out how much money you are making out of the deal, but don't be intimidated into walking away from this deal; stay in for the long haul and finish it.

Chapter 45

How to Foreclose on Properties

THERE ARE MANY WAYS to foreclose on properties. The best and most profitable way is to purchase a tax sale certificate, wait the allotted time, and foreclose on it. First, you go to a tax sale and bid on a tax sale certificate—that's when somebody doesn't pay their property taxes, or water, or sewer bill. The property goes up for tax sale, usually one day a year for each town. Get a list of the tax sales on line or from the individual townships.

You must pay all the subsequent taxes on the property after you buy the tax sale certificate (like you own it). The township will pay you 18 to 25 percent interest on the certificate and all the subsequent taxes you pay until either the owner redeems it or you foreclose on it.

Every state is different, but in a lot of states, it's two years to foreclose after you buy the tax sale certificate. After the two-year period, you hire a lawyer and start the foreclosure. It usually takes six to nine months to foreclose on a property, to get final judgments, and after that, the owner has three months to redeem his or her property back.

This is the cheapest way you can get a property, other than if the person gives the quitclaim deeds to you. You would hand the guy a couple of thousand dollars, and he would hand over the quitclaim deeds for the property to you. If the person is losing the property anyway, if the bank is foreclosing or whatever, you give him the money and he hands you the keys. At this point, you assume all responsibility for the property from the bank or whoever else is involved with the property. The third way to get a property is to go to a sheriff sale, and when somebody bids on the property, the owner has ten days to redeem the property. Go to the owner and give him some money and acquire the quitclaim deed for the property from him, and then go redeem it as the new owner. The tax sale certificates are guaranteed by the township to you if you go through all the procedures properly.

Of course, the old way is to just go up to the guy who is losing his house in a foreclosure action and give him some money and he hands you the keys. Make sure you run a title search on the property because you are assuming all his debts when you take the house, so you know exactly what you will owe in total.

You can make deals with everybody involved with the house. The guy that's holding the second mortgage, make a deal to discount that. The first mortgage, make a deal to discount that and get the whole deal down to where you want it. Make sure, whenever you make a deal, you get it in writing and have it notarized.

Once again, you must do the research in the state you're into, read the status, and make sure you know what you can and can't do. If you foreclose successfully on a property, you will make a lot of money when you sell the property, or you can keep the property and rent it out and let the tenants pay the mortgage off for you.

You can also purchase tax sale certificates from people who have purchased them at the tax sale. Maybe, for whatever reason, they want to sell them, so they put a premium on it and sell it to you for a small profit. The tax sale certificate could be a year old, two years old, and ready to foreclose on, or already in foreclosure. The closer it is to foreclosure, the more you will pay or maybe not.

Maybe, for whatever reason, the guy wants to sell. Of course, purchasing the tax sale certificates is a ball game all by itself. You will get a healthy interest rate if you just purchase them with no intention of foreclosure. Who's going to pay you 18 percent plus interest on anything these days?

The other way to foreclose is to call all the banks, get an REO list (real estate owned) from the banks, and find out what's available out there. Remember, nothing is written in stone. You can always negotiate a better deal than those they offer you. It depends who you're talking to and what they would like to accomplish.

Chapter 46

How to Purchase Business Cheap, Build Them Up, and Sell Them

For many years after I started my business brokerage, I found insolvent business and purchased them after I would list them and not be able to sell after six months. The average business that I purchased was for probably 25 percent of what it was worth. I would then put in a management team, pump up the business, and then sell it for four times what I paid for it.

I once purchased a pizza place for $15,000 and sold it for $75,000 in one week. The guy that purchased the place for $75,000 gave me a deposit of $15,000, which I actually used to purchase the place with. I was able to clear $60,000 in cash in one week. I already had the buyer when I purchased the place. The seller was from one of the Middle Eastern countries and had a hard time making the place go.

When you purchase a business, which includes real estate, it's good to move the business into a better location with lower rent, if you can find a place. Then take the building and convert its use and sell it to a developer after you've gotten the approvals to convert it into whatever you feel is the highest and best use.

For example, I purchased a day-care center, which was in a house next to city hall. I moved the day-care center into another location, put a management team in to build it up, and sold it for a nice profit. Because the property was next to city hall, I made the house a law firm for two young lawyers, which I found in the local university law school. I then formed an LLC and wound up owning 51 percent of the law firm. (What a lucrative project that turned out to be.)

Probably the easiest business to take over would be a dollar store that is insolvent. You can purchase where it shows a profit and then sell it for five times the net profit that you show. Another way to make money is to buy an insolvent business and break it up and sell off the pieces, kind of like buying automobiles and selling the parts.

A few years ago, I saw a movie called Pretty Woman with Julia Roberts and Richard Gere. Richard Gere played a self-made millionaire who purchased large businesses (mostly manufacturers), broke up the plant, sold off the equipment, and then developed the waterfront property into single units of detached and semidetached houses for families, professional sites, and a shopping mall. I got the idea from the movie and started a company to do exactly that.

Whatever kind of project you find, you make it work for yourself, and remember, if you don't have the money, you can syndicate the project.

Chapter 47

Taking Over Large Business from the Bank That Are in Bankruptcy

You can go into the bankruptcy court and look for large companies that are in trouble. There will be a large choice of various types of businesses for sale because the judge always wants to throw a business into chapter 7, once the owner decides to enter into chapter 11 (a reorganization plan).

The trustee can say the person is behind in their insurance premium or that they are late on their mortgage payment and easily convince a judge or to throw the man into chapter 7. When this happens, it's a heartbreak for the person that's losing a business that took him ten years to build up. The trustee gets 3 percent of whatever the business sells for in bankruptcy court, so he doesn't care that the man is losing his life's dream and probably won't ever get a chance to build up another business because the trustee will most likely ruin his credit while he's at it.

The trustee will take over the business and everything stops, the government taxes the guy owes, the state taxes, etc. The man loses 100 percent of everything once he throws himself on the mercy of the bankruptcy court. For the owner, it's a great loss, but for those who want to pick up the spoils and take off the windfall, it's a great deal.

Remembering that you have no money, you are going to have to plan the strategy. If you will go into a large deal like this, you must plan where the money is coming from. The first thing you want to do is open a web site on your computer and let people know that you're in the business of buying large bankrupt businesses, and you either take them over and run them, or buy them and sell off the pieces. Remember, the pieces can be worth more than the whole, like selling car parts.

Then you can go in and make a deal with the bankruptcy judge or the trustee of the bank to purchase the deal with some kind of creative financing because everybody's going to lose if the business doesn't sell. You can even raise money to help the guy out. Maybe he stays involved and maybe runs the business for your group; maybe he ran into financial trouble, it wasn't that he was a bad operator. Check things out.

Make sure you feel very comfortable with the deal. Check everything out and make sure that the deal will work for you. Maybe you move the business into a better location and develop the property for its highest and best use, whatever that is. This is just another way to create wealth for yourself.

Chapter 48

Foreclosing on Properties Using Adverse Possession

ADVERSE POSSESSION IS DEFINED as not founded by written instrument. An action for the recovery of real estate and a defense or counterclaim on title to real estate is barred by uninterrupted adverse possession of twenty years.

A person, who, in connection with his or her predecessors in interest, is in uninterrupted adverse possession of real estate for twenty years, may commence an action to establish title under Ch. 841. Real estate is possessed adversely under this section.

However, unfortunately for tax sale investors, the twenty-year prescriptive period makes this approach unattractive, especially for investors wishing to get rich quick by buying and immediately selling the property.

However, someone who is just interested in buying a home for pennies on a dollar might be willing to wait out the twenty-year period. This is a shorter period than the length of most mortgages today.

This approach might be interesting to a young investor who is looking for a home that can be turned into cash later in life. If the property is abandoned, then in effect, he or she is giving the real estate away. Any offer for just pennies on a dollar might be viewed by that owner as found money. Look for houses that are deemed as a house that could be taken by adverse possession.

Drive around, walk around, and look for properties that are neglected and unoccupied. When you find one, come back several times and see if there is ever anyone there. Days, nights, weekends, are their lights on? Go up to the door someday. Ring the bell. If anyone answers, you can tell him or her why you're there and see if they are interested in selling the property or you can say you have the wrong home or pretend to be a traveling salesman going door to door.

If no one answers, go to county records. Find out who pays the taxes. If you really are interested in the property, then you can contact them and make an offer. If you find out that no one is paying the taxes, then find out how long they have been delinquent. Then go back to the property and talk to the neighbors. What do they have to say? How long has the property been vacant? Does anyone ever come around?

If you get the answers you want that indicates that the property has indeed been abandoned, then you pay the taxes. Pay up any back taxes and bring them current. Then take possession of the property. Put up a sign saying that you own it and that everyone else should keep out. Change the locks on the doors. Advertise the property as a rental. If no one challenges you, then you have an income-producing property with no monthly payments.

You can't borrow against it until you get the title, but it is free and clear. You pay only the property taxes and insurance. But that is not the best part. Most states have adverse possession laws, which allow people to take over abandoned properties and eventually claim title to them if the owner does not object within a specified period.

Generally, the person who wants to take over the property has to prove that it was abandoned and that he took it over and used it flagrantly, openly, and in a manner hostile to the interest of the owner. Put it in simple English, this means you have to use the property openly and in a way that threatens the owner's ownership and control. Sneaking in these at night and then sneaking out again every morning won't do it, not even living there openly.

You have to challenge the owner's claim in some way. Putting up a sign advertising yourself as owner will establish your claim. You can put a fence around the property and do other things to discourage others from going onto the property. If the owner cares, he must respond to your actions.

He should send you a registered letter or, better yet, have his lawyer send it, warning you to stay away from his property or face legal action. If this happens, you are pretty well beaten. About all you can get out of it is save money you put up for property taxes and or improvements.

If the owner doesn't want to refund your money, you can always threaten to put a lien on the property. If you prove that you paid the taxes and/or improvements, you can put a cloud on the title. He will not be able to sell the property or borrow any money on it until the lien is cleared up.

Chapter 49

Going into Business for Yourself

I NEVER WORKED FOR anyone in my whole life. Either I was under independent contract with large corporations or I was in business for myself. So I can tell you firsthand how to go about it. Joining the self-employed is a big step for most people, to leave the security of a good job and take a shot at owning your own business. About 75 percent of businesses fail in the first five years, so how do you succeed where so many fail?

You want to be part of the 25 percent, the ones that make it, with sweat and tears, a lot of luck and hard work, unwavering courage, and mastery of detail. Important in a new business venture, any size, is to investigate the business idea itself and your own abilities to run the new business. Look at the product you're selling and see if it has a realistic chance to succeed in the marketplace.

It's important that you have the knowledge and skills to handle the accounting, marketing, advertising, legal, and private matters. You must make a formal business plan for your own use and for the use of any bank or lending institution that you may deal with. Most importantly, you must investigate the capability of the individuals who will manage, receive rewards, and share the losses with you. Make sure you have knowledge about the business and not just about the product itself.

You must be able to trust the people who are doing your bookwork and accounting. You've heard the stories about bookkeepers taking the business over. Make sure you have good, hardworking, honest people around you. As far as the legal papers required to start a business, find out whether you want a sole proprietorship or an LLC. Talk to a good attorney about what you want to do. Contact city, county, and state to see what specific licenses are required for your type of business.

It is necessary to have many legal documents executed also. You should have an accountant, a good lawyer, and maybe even a business adviser to ensure that your company is in compliance with city, state, and government law. In many cases, advertising suggests guaranteed success or that anyone can be successful in business; all businesses should be investigated —should be highly suspected. Most of the time, the only people who make money on deals are the ones that are selling them. If you do not understand starting a business, contact the Better Business Bureau.

The easiest to establish is the sole proprietorship. The owner is responsible for all the liabilities and places his or her personal assets on the line. A partnership is similar to a sole proprietorship, except that more than one person is involved in the profit sharing or management.

The other choices are the C or Regular Corporation and the S corporation. The difference between the two is in the taxation. In the C corporation, the entity is liable for income taxes on gross profits before distributions go to stockholders. The amount of profit leftover after paying corporate income tax is then distributed to the stockholders as dividends and is again taxable to the individual as income. So the profits of the C corporation are taxed twice.

In the S corporation, no corporate income taxes are paid and the profits are distributed to the stockholders in the year earned. The individual stockholders then pay personal income tax on those profits. The single most compelling reason for a corporation is to protect the personal assets of the corporation's stockholders. You should have a business plan to give the interested parties a five-year projection of what your company will make in the next five years.

A projected performance of how much money you will make in the next five years and how you intend to do it.

You can speak to a business broker to get a price as to what to sell your projects for. If I hired employees to work in my business, they would have an independent contractor's agreement drawn by me, spelling out their duties. This way, you don't have to withhold any income taxes; every person pays their own taxes.

Chapter 50

How to Syndicate an Energy Windmill Company to Supply Electricity to Small Cities

THERE ARE MANY SMALL cities that you could hook up electricity to and receive money, a utility fee, from the users. General Electric makes these windmills available to small companies that want to be in the electric supply business.

Once again, you put an ad in the paper, advertising, "Syndication for windmill-powered energy. Minimum investment of $50,000. Call for appointment." You at this point have gotten all the information on windmill energy that you can get and decided that you are going to put the windmills, after talking to the townships, hopefully down the shore were the winds blow strongest.

You have to contact General Electric, who makes the windmills, and then you decide where, and then you're going to ask if you can put them there. Do a cost and expense sheet and then find out which government agency will finance them for you and go from there.

The following are information about windmills:

A century of policies, subsidies, regulations, and rules have been built around fossil and nuclear resources and large hydro. These all need to be changed if we are to successfully promote climate solutions like comprehensive efficiency gains and solar, wind, governmental, and bio wastes.

A dozen or so individual states have taken faster action than the federal government, but it appears things are picking up steam. This is most obvious in wind power. Now operational in more than seventy countries, wind power had been the fastest source of renewable energy.

Worldwide wind power expanded more than fifteen-fold over the course of the decade, from 4,800 megawatts (MW) in 1995 to installed wind capacity 74,000 MW by the end of 2006. The wind market grew a record 41 percent in 2005, and despite supply-clean constraints in 2006, it achieved an impressive $32 growth. Some 150,000 people now employed in the global wind industry were responsible for the twenty-three billion in new generated equipment installed in 2006.

Europe still leads the market, with nearly fifty thousand MV installed capacity, representing 65 percent of the global total, and producing roughly one hundred billion kilowatt-hours (KWH) of electricity consumption.

The countries with the highest total installed capacity are Germany (20,621 MW), Spain (11,615 MW), India (6,270 MW), Denmark (3,136 MW), and the United States (11,603 MW), thirteen countries around the world, with France and Canada reaching the threshold in 2006.

The cost of wind power has fallen drastically as the world market has expanded. Today's wind turbine produces eighty times more electricity per year at less than half the cost per unit (KWH) than its counterpart of two decades ago. At a good location, wind can compete with the cost of coal—or gas-fired power.

I think I've given you the idea. Now run with it.

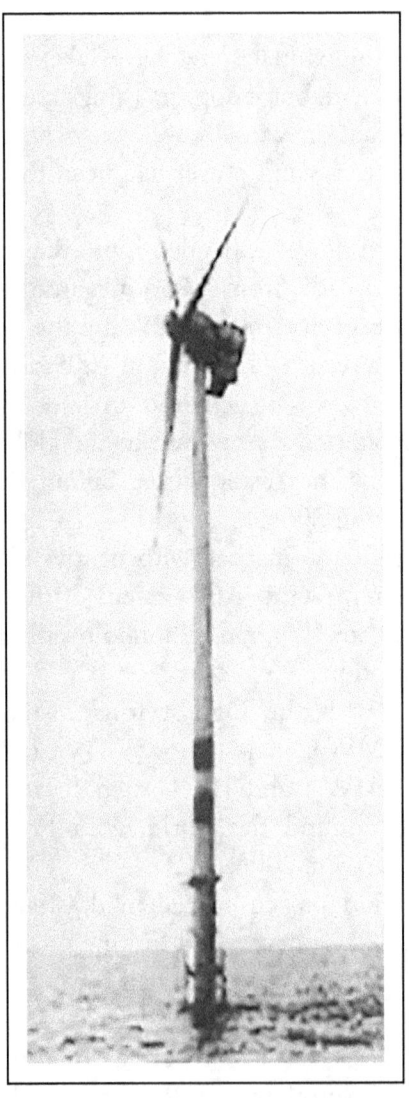

You're looking at the reason wind has become the fastest growing sector of the renewable energy market.

GE Energy has done it again with wind turbines that are almost inconceivable in size and efficiency. Both onshore and off, they give utilities and electric cooperatives an attractive energy solution with minimal environmental impact.

Chapter 51

How to Form a Real Estate Company with Syndication

You must first advertise for a real estate investment company to purchase and sell real estate. The minimum investment again is $50,000. Bring in as many people as you would like to own your real estate company but don't go over twenty-five. You can go after a franchise if you wish maybe Century 21 or Re-Max to give you a lot of assistance. Make your company a commercial industrial real estate company.

You are specializing in syndications, so you prefer to hire people who have that type of experience. Hire a good broker to manage your investment, one with, hopefully, fifteen or twenty years of experience in commercial industrial real estate. With the funds you receive from your syndication, rent or buy a nice small building to put your office in. Use your brokers' experience when you advertise; say how long you have been selling commercial industrial real estate.

You will have a meeting with your staff once a week for, hopefully, an hour or more. You will try to do some business brokerage business to help pay the bills. Listing and selling business is easy, and it creates revenue for your office. You will start the meeting saying, "One of you take the east side of the street, and one of you takes the west side of the street and see who gets the most business listings, business for sale." Offer a reward for the most business listed in a month. Teach your staff how to do syndications and send them out to find large buildings, apartment buildings, and shopping centers to purchase for your syndications. Have them tell the sellers that you are in the business of doing syndications and tell the seller that you'll get a higher price because you intend to convert his or her building into condominiums and create a profit for your group.

You will be able to use the commissions from these deals to finance some of the cost associated with putting syndication together. Hopefully, you won't need any of the commissions to help you, but you never know. Make all your staff independent contractors so you don't have to mess with withholding taxes from their commissions.

You should take at least 5 percent of your gross profit and put it back into advertising. Don't waste your advertising. Check it out each week before it goes into the newspaper or wherever you are advertising. Keep a close eye on where the funds that go in and out of your checking account go. Run a tight ship, and you can be a large commercial industrial brokerage while you're doing your syndications.

Chapter 52

How to Put a Factory Syndication Together

In order to put a factory deal together, you must decide what kind of factory you want to build, and hopefully, it's in a low-income area where the town is a state target area for low employment where you have a need for a factory. If the factory is in a target area that the state designates as such, the state will lend you a great deal of money at a very low interest rate, with a high percentage of the loan. In other words, they could lend you 110 percent of what you need.

In order to buy or build a factory, you must make a list of the employees you are going to have and include 50 percent minorities. Minorities could be students, housewives, or people who need the jobs the most. After you check out the area to see what is needed, you will submit this list to the state people who lends the money. In New Jersey, it's called the EDA or Economic Development Authority. It has a different name in every state, so check it out. In New Jersey, if the factory is in an EDA target area, you are more apt to get the loan.

Hopefully, you can find a building that already exists cheap, and the state will lend you the money to buy it, fix it up, and make whatever it is that you want it for where you are going to employ a lot of needy people.

The best factory that is in demand is one that manufactures something that is needed for consumption in the area. You might want to find out what kind of product is in demand in your area and check out the amount of need for that product. You might want to find out how much of an item is used and what the consumption of that item has been in recent years.

Then because you haven't any money, you're going to have to put together a syndication once you've done all your research. You must start the ball rolling if you want to make something out of this. So after you decide what you want to do, how you're going to finance this thing, then you will start making this deal work for yourself.

You will put an ad in the paper, saying, "Syndication manufacturing plant, minimum investment of $50,000, great investment, great write-offs." You want to contact people in the $200,000-plus income bracket because they need the most write-offs, and you will give them the write-offs on a five-year depreciation on equipment and fixtures.

It's almost like you get the money before they give it to the government. Now they get a chance to make even more money in the future. Now you make an agreement with them to buy them out; after five years, you will own 100 percent. You have five years' depreciation on furniture, fixtures, and equipment that you can give them, and they will divide it equally among themselves. And I think twenty-eight years on the real estate, twenty-eight divided by the value of the real estate.

Chapter 53

How to Be a Comedian, Make Friends and Audiences Laugh

YOU CAN PUT TOGETHER a series of jokes that you already know and some you have to find in joke books. You start out by telling a story about a certain subject and build the jokes into it. Did you ever want to be a very funny person who makes people laugh? Well, I've written a monologue that you could actually get up on a stage with and make people laugh.

It goes like this:

I'll never forget the day I was born. The doctor looked at my mother, my mother looked at my father, and the doctor said, "What are you going to name him?"

My father said, "I don't want to name him."

Somebody said, "You name him and you can have him."

"Well, I don't want him."

When I was three, my father called me into the den; we lived in a cave. My father said, "What do you want for Christmas, a boy or a girl?"

I said, "I want a watch," so they threw me out. My parents wanted me to leave home so bad, they used to pack my lunch in a road map; they used to tie a pork chop around my neck so the dog would play with me.

My mother and father moved when I was four, but I found them again when I was five. Then I grew older, and I met Sally; now, that's a girl. That's what my friends used to say, "That's a girl?" She had very affectionate eyes; the left eye kept looking at the right eye. She wasn't cross-eyed or anything, but when she cried, the tears ran down her back; she had back-teria.

I used to take her out on a date. I would grab her fur; I didn't know it was growing there. She had the most beautiful long black silky hair hanging from her armpits. I'll never forget the night we eloped in my 1946 Cushman motor scooter. We rode all night and finally found the little sign on the lawn, "Just a Piece."

I said, "How much to get married?"

He said, "How much you think she's worth?"

So I gave him fifty cents, he gave me a quarter back, and we got married. Then we went to the motel and did the usual things, played checkers. She said, "When are you going to leave me alone and jump me, man."

Afterward, I decided to take a bath. I filled up the tub with water, but the water leaked out. So I called room service, "I got a leak in my bathtub."

The guy said, "Go ahead, it's your room, you're paying for it."

The room was so small I stuck the key in the door, and the window was broken. You had to go outside to change your mind. I closed the bedroom door, and I was in bed with the doorknob. We went downstairs to see the floor show (there was a hole in the rug). There was a pretty girl up on the stage. I tried to catch her eye, but it rolled under the table, and the waiter got it.

Well, we've been home now for two weeks, and there's the pitter-patter of little feet around the house; my mother-in-law is a midget. But there's one thing about Sally, she really dresses to kill, and she cooks that way too. On weekends, most people have pot roast; we have roast pot. Even Sinatra wouldn't get anything out of her Wheaties.

Sally came up to me and told me she wanted a Volkswagen, but she didn't want me to spend the money, so she went out and bought

1,500 lbs. of steel and wood and kitted one. The first day she had it, I came home and found the car in the living room. I said, "How did you get the car in the living room?"

She said, "It's easy, when you get to the kitchen, you make a right."

Every night, I back the car in the garage, and the next morning, she backs it out.

A friend of mine saw her coming up Broad Street in Philadelphia; he ran five blocks up to the top of the PSFS building, and she hit him. Sally gets seven pedestrians per gallon. And luckily last week, she hit a guy and knocked him fifty feet, and the guy got a ticket for leaving the scene of the accident.

Chapter 54

How People Get Real Estate through Commercial or Civil Conspiracy

THE EASIEST TARGET FOR getting real estate by using conspiracy is to attack large restaurants with catering. A group of individuals from other countries who came over to the United States in the fifties decided to give the police and state police free coffee and, in some cases, free food. After doing this for many years, they decided to cash in and collect some of the money they put out.

They approached the state police, who was in charge in some states of the liquor-control boards, and they closed up a lot of restaurants that were operating so that these individuals could purchase them out of their bankruptcies and insolvency situations.

The largest restaurant in my state was closed while they were filing chapter 11 (reorganization plan), which is a way to get time to pay off your debtors over a five-year period. The restaurant was doing three million a year with one million dollars on the books for weddings. The local newspaper did a whole page ad about the chapter 11.

The restaurant that spent about 125,000 a year in advertising in the local paper was closed after thirty days, so the newspaper that created the bad press actually closed the restaurant.

Freedom of the press can be a killer for small businesses. If your daughter is getting married in May, you're going to move your wedding someplace else because the place may not be there. Not to mention that the state doesn't get any sales tax, and the amount of unemployment the state has to pay out of unemployment for one hundred employees, and of course, the government doesn't receive any income tax payments any more. So you see how a little thing like filing a chapter 11, the press can and will destroy the restaurant. So a place where somebody spent twenty-five years building lost about three million dollars just so the press could have its day.

Another place I can recall was closed up by the press when the state sales tax got six months behind. The state tax people tipped off the press that they were coming out to collect back taxes. The restaurant was sixty-five years old and doing $2.7 million a year. The owner immediately paid the back sales tax, but the press had to have their day. There was another million dollars on the books for the weddings; the fathers of the brides started to cancel the weddings. The restaurant again was closed thirty days after that.

What happened was that the restaurant was forced to file chapter 11 because the taxes were due, and at first, the owner didn't have the money to pay the taxes.

By the time the owner paid the taxes, it was too late. The owner filed chapter 11, and immediately, the trustee that was appointed went to the court and claimed the owner was behind in his fire insurance payment. The judge immediately gave a restaurant that was doing $2.7 million a year to the trustee to liquidate. The restaurant didn't even have a chance to save itself. The restaurant was recently appraised for $2.7 million was sold at auction for $1.2 million two months after the trustee moved in.

The trustee receives 3 percent of the sale price when he sells a restaurant, so the trustee was not going to let that money slip by. Additionally, the attorney for the debtor, the attorney for the unsecured creditors, and all the other attorneys involved all moved in like vultures and gobbled up the carcass of the poor man that owned the place who didn't see this all coming.

A third place was forty years old and a beautiful place. A man came in one night and had dinner and took the leftovers home. He ate them a week later and got sick. He complained to the board of health, who went out to this 15,000-sq.-ft. restaurant, and they found two roaches and they closed the place for one week. They had again one million dollars on the books for weddings that year, and again, the fathers of the brides scurried to move the wedding.

Once again, the place never opened again. Now this site has a large high-rise sitting on it. Doesn't it make you wonder if the whole thing was a put-up job so that someone could get the land for a song?

Chapter 55

The Master of Mirrors

WHEN I FIRST GOT started in my real estate brokerage, I developed an image of being a master of mirrors. I was able to get people that had more credibility than I had to kind of represent me in my ventures, people that had some kind of control over people with money, people who knew people that had the wherewithal to enter into my kind of deals and make them work.

At first, I contacted many accountants, lawyers, bank managers, presidents of large companies, insurance brokers, and the principals of larger real estate companies than mine and sold them on the idea that what I was selling was what people wanted to buy. I always paid a finder's fee to these people who I used to contact other people with.

You will find it's easier to open doors using the right people to get in with. I contacted large commercial industrial real estate companies first to sell their businesses for them, which they didn't want to handle themselves. After I got to know them and I won their favor, I got them to put large offers on warehouses and shopping centers that I wanted to syndicate because they had the creditability to get the deals accepted under my terms with many contingencies.

I used accountants to introduce to their clients who were investors who would come into my deals. I used insurance company brokers to introduce me to their clients who had millions of dollars of real estate insured with their company. Whenever I was selling tax sale certificates or tax sale certificate syndications, I used bankers to sell them for me, paying them a nice finder's fee to introduce me to their customers. To use everybody's credibility to meet others is the best way to break the ice and get in a big deal. When you are putting together a big deal, it is good to find credible people who are experienced in the particular field that you are putting syndication together on.

For example, if you're pulling a syndication together on a large restaurant, find experienced restaurant managers that are strong enough to get in the deal and run it for you after you're involved with it. After all, you're going to be involved at least five years. Basically, by getting people to introduce their clients to you for money is one way to get some people's interest in helping you foster. What you're doing is getting people to use their credibility; money is the root of all evil, and everybody wants to get in on the action.

I found out that this method is the most effective way to get the job done, and it lasts a lot longer if you do it the right way. In putting together large syndications for years, I found out that choosing the right people is important. Putting anybody in a deal just for the sake of making the deal is crazy if you want the deal to be successful long term.

Remember, you're going to buy everybody out after five years and own the whole company, so you want it to be good. Remember, you don't have to be a real estate broker to put any large deals together. In fact, you're better off if you're not. The real estate commission is looking for ways to put you out of business, if they can, especially when you're dealing with other professionals and getting involved with finder's fees and so on.

In fact, I have an ex-employee who got a broker's license and went into business for himself, and he puts his commission back in every deal for the buyer's down payment. The last time I checked, he had a $15,000 a month income from that alone.

Chapter 56

How to Get Real Estate by Heir Hunting, Deed Raiding, and Redemption without Cause

BEFORE YOU TRY ANY of these kinds of actions, check the laws in your state; you don't want to break the law. There are many ways to get real estate by heir hunting, and the most common way is to call the person who is in foreclosure and ask them how much they want to walk away from their house. The owner hands you the keys and you hand them a check. They sign a simple quitclaim deed, and that's it: you own the house for better or for worse.

You may want to run a search on the property to see how many other liens are against the property because you are going to have to pay everything off if the person who is foreclosing on the house didn't already do so. But then you own the property. You might want to check in your state what the laws are about heir hunting too; make sure everything you do is legal. You're going to get some flak from the person who is foreclosing, but if you're not doing anything wrong, don't worry about it.

Remember, it doesn't make a difference how big the property is or whether it is commercial, industrial, or professional; it's all real estate. The bigger the property is, the more you will make on it. If it's a large property, you can change the use to the highest and best use and make even more money on it. Change a warehouse into self-storage, change a hotel into hotel condominiums, a shopping center into condominium stores, or whatever.

Deed raiding is going to a sheriff sale, and when somebody bids on a house and wins, the person that is losing the house has ten days to redeem it. You call up the person who is losing the house, make an appointment with them and sit down with them, offer them some money, and have them sign a quitclaim deed. Let them give you the keys and then go in and redeem it with the county. The county will give the money back to the person who bid on the property at the sheriff's sale, then you now own the house. Again, make sure you run a title search to find out what other liens are against the property.

Make sure you find out who the heirs are by checking the deed and find out if somebody died and left the house to them. Once you know who you are dealing with, run with it. The last way is to call the person that's foreclosing on the house, and you give him an amount of money, contingent upon foreclosing on the house, and buy him out. If the person lives fifty to seventy-five miles away and the property is near you, then you have more negotiating power.

Again, you want to run a title search to determine how much is owed on the property. You can also call the bank. Now if the owner doesn't pay, you can foreclose yourself. If the bank, say, has a $70,000 mortgage, offer them $25,000, etc. If there is a second mortgage for $40,000, offer them $10,000 for that. If someone else is foreclosing on the property, it could be trouble for the bank, and they would rather write it off.

Redemption without cause is made by an investor who will go to a tax sale and buy a tax lien. After the complaint has been filed and the tax lien is being foreclosed, someone who is not involved in the foreclosure will go out and attempt to acquire a prior tax lien, an old mortgage on a property, or a deed to the property and then attempt to either compel the foreclosing lien holder to assign its interest or redeem out the lien holder. If the foreclosing lien holder gives in and assigns his interest, normally, the interloper will take away from the foreclosing lien holder most of the profit in the foreclosure.

Chapter 57

How to Make One Million Cash Tax Free on One Deal by Buying Real Estate

I HIRED A SALESMAN about twenty years ago to sell real estate, and he told me he would purchase the real estate and use his commission for the down payment, and I said, "I have no problem with that." The man would look for the deals that were undervalued and negotiate the deal down even further until the deal was worth about 60 percent of its value.

The man would purchase the property, then go to the bank for a loan and borrow 80 percent loan to value from the bank and pocket the 20 percent. If the man purchased a $100,000 property, then he would put $20,000 in his pocket, then have the tenants pay 100 percent of the loan off for him. I didn't realize it at the time, but the 20 percent of the deal that he was putting in his pocket was tax free. Why? Because he borrowed the money; it wasn't earned income.

Then somewhere down the line, he would recapture the taxes, mostly when he sold the property at the end, less the depreciation of five years on furniture and fixtures and thirty-one-year level term depreciation, which was taken off. The man purchased eight properties from me before he got his own broker's license and went into business for himself. Today, the man is a billionaire living in California.

I recently got a call from a bank in Florida that had two large condominium properties that they had financed. They had thirty units left in one and twenty-eight units left in the other; the bank wanted out of the deal. The units were selling from between $118,000 per unit to $196,000 per unit, depending on the size.

I called my clients in Brooklyn, and they purchased them all for about $60,000 per unit, about half of their value, amounting to about $7.8 million, then turned around and went to the bank and borrowed ten million dollars; it was a little less than their value. That put over two million in cash in their pocket, tax free because they borrowed the money, it wasn't earned income. Again now, the tenants will pay off the mortgage for them and they will make a little profit on that, plus they took over the condo associations, which were also very lucrative.

So you now understand how to put a lot of cash in your pocket without paying taxes on it. Remember, if you can tie up this deal under contract, then you can assign the deal to someone else and let them settle for a fee or go to the bank yourself and borrow the money. The bank isn't going to look at your credit too much; they're going to look at the deal. When it's in the millions, the bank will look at the deal only.

Chapter 58

How to Syndicate New Jersey Tax Sale Certificates and Gain up to 25 Percent Interest in Properties with No Money

You first put an ad in the local newspaper, saying, "Syndication, tax sale certificates, minimum investment of $10,000." When you receive calls back, you set up a meeting and meet with your investors. You get five people to put up $10,000 each to invest. You can do a conference call with me, and I will explain to your investors how everything works.

You buy from me ten tax sale certificates for $50,000 that is two years old and ready to foreclose on. If you foreclose on strictly vacant boarded-up houses, you will get about 10 percent of what you foreclose on.

Make sure that you record these tax certificates in the county that they're from, and make sure that you pay all the subsequent water, sewer, and property taxes due each quarter and file an affidavit with the township as to what you paid, until you foreclose on the properties.

If the property is redeemed by the property owner or the mortgage company, they will pay you 18 percent interest on whatever you have spent for subsequent taxes paid and 18 percent on whatever amount the certificate is worth with the township.

Remember, you can always have the bank assign the mortgage to you, then you become the bank.

I would charge my investors 25 percent ownership in the properties for putting the syndication together, managing the lawyer's foreclosures, and managing the properties afterward.

As you receive these properties, immediately apply for permits from the township and start renovating. After the properties are finished, you can refinance them and pull out 80 percent loan to value so you can keep the money and get your renters to pay your mortgages off. This will give your investors a quick return on their money, usually about a year turnaround.

So let's see now: you invested $50,000, you got one $150,000 back home that you spent $50,000 remodeling. You made $50,000 profit in one year for your investors and yourself, 25 percent of that nets you $12,500 in one year with no money, and you still own 25 percent of the property afterward, which will appreciate.

If you're interested in pursuing this, contact Bob Domico at Domico Investments at 609-792-7593. I will give you more information about tax sale certificates that's not in my book. If you are very lucky, you'll get two houses back, then you double your profit. Remember, you can do that ten times in one year.

Chapter 59

You're Better Off with No State Licenses If You're Doing My Deals

IF YOU HAVE A real estate broker's license when you're doing some of my deals, it's not good. The state frowns upon giving money to accountants and attorneys for turning over clients to you so you can do your syndications, etc. You're better off not having any kind of license in your state.

If you're a real estate broker, you can't very well throw your commission back into the deal to make it work. For example, if the buyer doesn't have enough to put down on the deal, you lend him the money.

You're better off being a business broker. In most states, they don't require a license, and an example would be if you were to throw your commission back into a deal, when you list the business and not the real estate, it's as follows: the building is worth one million dollars and the business is worth one million dollars, you list the business and not the real estate.

You're only going to get paid on the business half, say 10 percent, so you're only going to make $100,000, rather than $200,000. So you lend the buyer $100,000. That's only $20,000 a year that you get back, plus interest, that isn't bad. Now you can go ahead with your deal. You don't have to worry about whether or not you lose your license.

My whole book is about bringing people, accountants, lawyers, real estate brokers, many forms of professionals, which you couldn't do if you're licensed. Why do you want state-enforced representatives checking everything you do with a fine-tooth comb?

Some of the things you will do in my book are borderline legal. You will probably get sued a few times because someone will say you're making too much on brokering tax sale certificates or assigning a property or flipping a piece of real estate. These things are merchantable items. You can make $5,000 on a car, $10,000 on a boat, $20,000 on a plane, and $50,000 on a piece of real estate. No matter what you do, some guy is going to say you're committing fraud. As long as you do nothing illegal and you don't have any state licenses, you're good to go.

Once again, before you do anything, check with a good attorney to make sure it's legal; every state is different. An example would be purchasing property and not paying any mortgages or losing a property in foreclosure and then buying it back from the guy that foreclosed on it and so on. This is what I mean by borderline legal.

If you have any kind of state license and you lose it, you will be in the same category as a disbarred attorney or someone who got fired for taking a bribe, like a code enforcement officer in town. Once you get painted with that brush, everyone will be afraid to deal with you.

If you have any kind of state license, give it up while you're doing my deals. If they don't work out, you can always get it back later. But for now, listen to the master of mirrors and do what he says.

Chapter 60

Foreclosure

In 2008, we had 1.2 million foreclosures in the US, and before the end of 2010, we are supposed to go up to 8.2 million foreclosures. The government has asked the banks and mortgage companies to help with the situation. The banks must reduce the amounts of mortgages by at least 10 percent and reduce interest rates to around 5 percent to save the economy. Many banks have agreed to help.

You first need about ten square feet of office space, with about ten desks to get started. You can open it yourself or you can form a syndication to get started. The idea is to hire an attorney to contact the homeowner's mortgage company and ask them to knock 10 percent off the total amount of your mortgage and reduce your mortgage interest rate to around 5 percent.

If you are in the rears with your mortgage payments, try to push the late payments to the end of your loan. This will give the homeowners a change to hold on to their home, instead of letting their home go into foreclosure. It cost a lot of money for a mortgage company to foreclose and they really don't want to do it.

So now you come along and start a home loan modification company and help these people save their home. Do you think you would get any takers to help them save their mortgage? I think so. After you set your office and find your attorney to help you, the attorney should charge you about $500 per mortgage to take your client through the mortgage modification process.

You will then hire some people on commission only, hopefully people in the mortgage business, realtors, and anybody who has a previous knowledge about mortgages. After all, their business has slowed up quite a bit also because of this bad economy. Now they have a chance to make as much as $2,000 per week doing home loan modifications.

You will go online and find a company who has set up a website that asks the customers if they are losing their home, are behind their payments, and if they need help with contacting their mortgage company to reduce their mortgage payments. Of course, you will pay a fee for each customer that they gave you. This will give time to set up your own website, so you don't have to pay for the leads anymore.

After you set up your office with a telephone system, ten computers, an answering machine, and so on, you will train a couple of processors to call your clients so that the lawyer will charge you less. The processors will also be on commission.

The commission you will pay your salespeople will usually be about 20 percent of the fee charged to the homeowner. The amount of fee you will charge the homeowner is usually one month of mortgage payment.

Many people are taking advantage of this business because there is such a need for it. Be careful only to charge an application fee upfront because things may move a little slow and you will get complaints made to the attorney general's office. People are quick to complain if you ask them for the whole amount that you're charging them upfront, even though you are doing them a big favor. They won't see it that way; after all, they're broke and behind in their mortgage and they are a little desperate, as far as how fast you can move on saving their house. Just remember that they need you more than you need them.

Chapter 61

Mortgage Cash Flow Notes, Another Business for the Coming Bad Times

When someone sells a house themselves, not being able to sell it any other way, and the buyer for whatever reason can't get financing, then the seller is forced to hold a mortgage themselves. This is called a purchase money mortgage. The buyer is a good payer of the monthly mortgage; he has a good job and so on, but was not able to get a mortgage.

Getting a mortgage today is very difficult: you need a high credit score; otherwise, your interest rate will be too high.

The person who sold the house wanted to get cash but was forced to hold a mortgage for the buyer. Now the person, for whatever reason, wants their money out, maybe to buy another property, maybe to go into business—for whatever reason they want their money out.

In this situation, the seller, who is now the holder of the mortgage, is willing to discount the mortgage to get their money out. Your new company will list the mortgage for sale, advertise it, and sell it to another party for more money than the person who is selling it is asking, making you a profit. For example, the seller sold their house for $100,000. He took $20,000 down and financed $65,000; now he wants his money out.

He is willing to take $65,000 for the mortgage. You advertise the mortgage for sale $70,000; you just made $5,000 profit. If you do four times a week, you will make a million a year.

Other types of funds such as someone who gets an endowment or some kind of pay-out settlement or hits the lottery and gets so much a month, but now they want their cash out. These types of things are called cash flow notes. When someone wants to get their money and are willing to discount the notes, that's where you make your profit: by listing the note for sale and making profit on the transaction.

As you go along, the tighter the economy gets, the more business you will do. You can create a website to advertise your cash flow mortgage notes for sale, and the buyers and seller of these mortgage notes will call you. Your business will take off like nobody's business.

You just have to take the first step to make it happen, and guess what, you don't need any money to start this business; all you need is a cell phone and a place with a desk.

The buyers of these notes can be banks, mortgage companies, private investors, or anybody with money to buy them. If you want to, you could put together a syndication to raise money to buy the notes, and now you're getting a percentage of the syndication for putting it together, you're getting a percentage to manage the deal, and you're making your commission too. Wow, what a deal.

You can easily make a million a year out of this deal with no money. Don't wait another day; start this company tomorrow. Good luck from the master of mirrors.

My friends and clients up in New York tagged me with the name the Master of Mirrors because only I can put a deal together when the odds on making the deal are totally against me.

Domico writes about all the tricks of the trade, cunning techniques, and borderline legal methods of putting real estate deals together from scratch with no money. He will explain to you, the reader, how to purchase a two- to five-million-dollar piece of real estate, syndicate it, and own it yourself in five years, all with no money of your own.

The Master of Mirrors will show you step by step how to use the other people's credibility to purchase these large pieces of real estate and receive all the benefits yourself.

Chapter 1

Putting Together a Rooming House

WHEN I GOT OUT of the service at age twenty-one, I decided I was going to make my fortune in real estate. So with my discharge pay, I purchased a large house with seven bedrooms and two bathrooms and made my first rooming house. I converted the porch and the dining room into two more bedrooms, making a total of nine bedrooms, which I rented out in whose days for $50 a week each. I didn't give anyone use of the kitchen, and I didn't allow anyone to have company; you just went directly to your rooms and basically went to sleep, and that was it. I allowed no food in rooms or any loud noise after 10 p.m. It was a great place if you had a job and you were making minimum wage.

My mortgage payment was $250 a month, my electric bill was $165, my gas bill averaged $150 a month, all year round. Because I had a well and septic tank, even getting them pumped out and serviced a couple times a year only cost me an average of $35 a month. My insurance ran me only $50 a month, about $25 a month for maintenance, so the expenses were $670 per month. My income was $1,330 a month on my first property net.

There I was, back in the late 1950s, making over $17,000 a year, not working for anybody. It was very important to get a lot of information about your tenants, such as next of kin, mother and father's name and address, social security number, employer's name, landlord history, last job, etc. I always had an application ready for them to fill out. That way, if they do any damage to your property, you can chase them down.

I remember growing up with the Kennedy family who never sold anything they ever bought, just kept passing real estate down from one generation to the next. This is the theory I used my whole life to obtain great wealth. I heard so many of the old-timers saying, "If only I never sold anything that I ever bought, I would be rich today." I always remembered that old rule of thumb, and it kept me going for years.

The average income in the late 1950s was about $10,000 a year, and here I was, barely twenty-one years old, making almost double that amount. It was a good thing I had my shipping-out pay from the navy to buy this property.

To make my property even more secure, I put three locks on each door. In case someone didn't pay the rent on time, I would lock the other two locks so that they wouldn't be able to get into their room because they only had the key to the middle lock, not the top and bottom one. I then installed an old drop safe in the foyer so they would drop their rent in at the end of the week, so I didn't have to be there every day.

This system is a good way to get started in the real estate business because in today's market, where real estate isn't too good, you can buy cheap, like maybe do a short sale and with first-time home buyers' discount, put 3 percent down or less and be able to create your immediate income by purchasing a home now.

Today's income would be $100 a week for that room instead of $50 a week, which would give you $900 a week or $4,050 a month for the nine rooms. It would net you over $3,000 a month or $36,000 a year. That's as much as half of the people in the United Sates are making and on your first real estate deal. Wow. Just go into the multiple listing services and start looking for a short sale on a large house today. Begin your journey into the world of real estate today; you won't be sorry.

Chapter 2

Converting Residential Zoning into Professional Zoning or Highest and Best Use

THE NEXT THING I did was to purchase a large house next door to a large city hall in a small town in New Jersey. I decided to make it a law firm by pulling out the two bathtubs and making them into powder rooms. I also took out the kitchen and made it a conference room. I converted a five-bedroom house into a five-office law building. I advertised in the newspaper of the local law school and got only two young lawyers to come in and rent this house-building for their new law offices. I decided to form my own law firm.

I formed an LLC (Limited Liability Company) and started my own law firm, with the two lawyers as partners. I was the general partner, and they were limited partners. I owned 52 percent and they owned 49 percent. I contacted two young attorneys who had just graduated law school. I told them that down south, in Virginia and Maryland, the law firms are all located close to courthouses, and every week that they have court, all they have to do is go in and give out their cards.

They took my advice, and now they always have several hundred cases going all the time. Every Thursday night, there's always 150 traffic tickets given out on the nearby highway, and there are always domestic cases and criminal cases going on. Last year, the rent was $30,000 as opposed to the $12,000 a year if it were a house. The net was over $100,000 to me alone, using a 10 percent capitalization rate. It makes the building and business worth over a million dollars compared to a $100,000 house which it was before. We actually increased the value of this property ten times what it was before. The idea of a law firm next to a courthouse is an excellent way to increase the value of real estate.

This type of a real estate deal is called highest and best use, taking something that is worth one amount and making it much more valuable by changing the use to a higher and better use. We will get into this in another chapter of this book. We will teach you how to turn many different properties into highest and best use.

If you are good enough to find highest and best-use properties for other people, you will have the best and highest paying job in the world. If you can find a property, change the use and make it worth five to six or seven times more valuable; you can just imagine what worth you would have. Here in this book, we will show you how to do it. To be able to purchase a piece of real estate and make it worth so many times more than what you bought it for is the most wonderful feeling in the world, so read on and we'll tell you how it's done. We will take you from the basics of land and buildings and show you everything there is to know about everything where real estate is concerned. Learn all you can about highest and best use, and your fortune will be just around the corner. You must find your niche and pursue it to the ultimate. People have been, for many years, taking something that somebody else thinks is not valuable and making it worth a fortune.

Just remember, it only takes one of the deals that I am talking about in this book to get you off to a good start, then from there, everything is coming up roses. To define highest and best use, take a restaurant that takes up a whole block downtown, say it's worth three million dollars. On all four sides are high-rise buildings that are worth forty million each; what would you do with that restaurant?

Knock it down and build another forty-story high-rise. Surely, you can find a warehouse or a building that you can see a higher use in its place; you only have to look and use your imagination.

Chapter 3

Putting Together a Shopping Center from Scratch Is Easier Than You Think

You are riding down the street one day on a highway, and you see a piece of land about five acres; you pull over and close your eyes for a moment, and you see a fifty thousand square foot shopping center built on the large lot. You start to wonder how I am going to make this happen and what I can do next. Depending on location, the land is probably worth between $300,000 and $500,000. You call the owner up and ask him if he would like to sell the property and how much he would want for it.

You tell the owner that you would like to bring the property to the highest and best use, which would probably be a shopping center, but you won't know until you do more investigation in the area. You will tell the owner that you must do some borings on the land and run some demographics to see how much work is needed and what the area is like. You tell the owner that he has to give you the property for a year to find out what can be done on it.

You tell the owner, after all, McDonald's doesn't purchase a piece of land unless they can build a McDonald's on it. The owner has to be convinced that you have to get approvals to do what you want on the land to give for a year to get it approved. Tell the seller that you will put on his desk the work that you do on the property: the survey, the topographic studies, the borings, the setbacks, the conceptual, etc., as you go through the approval process, all received approvals. If, for any reason, you don't purchase the property from the owner, he will have a much more valuable property; here is why.

A property that is just land is known as the first value; after all, it's just the price of the unimproved land. But start getting the land through the approval process, and each time you get anything done, it increases the value of the property. For example, say a piece of land is worth $350,000. Then you are going to get borings done, setbacks, topographic studies done, and so on. An empty lot is worth say $350,000; an approved lot is worth $25 000 a foot approved for $1,250,000 or hire a contractor and build it yourself. The next value you will achieve is the value of the structure built; it's worth when empty is about $75 a square foot or $3,750,000, but when rented will be worth more like six or seven million. So you see, if you were to give it back to the seller at any given time, he would have a windfall. Now as long as you promise to give it back to him at any time if you don't buy it, he is going to make a lot of money from you. So you can see why he would give you the land upfront. Now where you are going to get the money to pay all these professionals that you're going to hire to get all these approvals for you? Well, basically, you have options. You could approach them on a basis of doing the work on a contingency, paying them double what they normally get if they hold out for payment. That wouldn't cost you that much, considering how much the property is going to appreciate and it would definitely decrease your risk.

Most probably you would go to a bank or EDS (Economic Development Authority) or the Small Business Administration and borrow the money to build the project. Now you have value 1 which is the land, value 2 which is the approved site, value 3 which is the building built, and value 4 which is the building fully rented. Wow, now you sell it to an investor or form syndication; we'll get into syndications in another chapter.

Chapter 4

Putting Together a Self-Storage Complex from an Existing Warehouse or Building from Scratch

YOU ARE RIDING DOWN a busy highway with 250,000 cars a day going by. You see a large warehouse 200,000 square feet. You decide right there and then that you're going to convert that warehouse into a self-storage complex, simply because there are 250,000 looking at that warehouse every day. You will purchase it and put a big sign on it: Cheap Self-Storage.

Now every day, 250,000 cars will see that sign as they're driving by. You convert that warehouse that is presently rented out for $600 a year and build 5×10 and 10×20 cages inside. You then rent the space out for the going rate which is $25 a foot a year. Say you pay $1.8 million for the warehouse; now it's worth seven million plus. This is called converting space into highest and best use. Once again, you will approach the owner and tell him that you need the property to convert it to its highest and best use, but don't tell the owner what that is or he will do it himself. Just tell him you are bringing the building to the highest and best use, but you're not sure what that is yet.

Let's run the numbers: allowing for 20 percent for hallways and passages, the cages will cover about 80 percent of the space. The area of the cages will be approximately 160,000 square feet;

at $25 a foot, that would be $400,000 a year income, as compared to the previous use at an income of approximately $100,000 a year. Four times the income will generate at least four times the value of the building now; instead of being worth $1.8 million, it's now worth $7.2 million. This is a prime example of highest and best use, changing a building into a higher use.

If you wanted to build a building from scratch, the same rule would apply. You would use a pre-constructed building like maybe from Butler Steel that was already made in a factory and delivered to the site, already constructed. The building would already have the cages built into it, and it would be delivered and ready to start having people move their contents inside. But of course, maybe you wouldn't have as good of a location with all those thousands of cars riding by every day.

There are many kinds of buildings you can use for this purpose in the city, but it must be one with a lot of visual exposure for the value to be there. After you get the building finished and ready to occupy, give the tenants a box truck free to move their stuff inside your building; offer a lower rate to get the building full, then raise the rate afterward. Once they get their stuff inside, they're not going to want to move their stuff again. Before you tackle this project, check the area and see how many homes don't have basements or extra storage areas. Check the demographics, and see how much of a need there is for this kind of building in this area.

Many different kinds of people need storage space. There are homeowners for one and then there are businesses of all types that need storage for various reasons. Perhaps a plumber that works out of his home needs storage for his supplies and equipment, someone who just bought a load of merchandise for a holiday, or someone who has moved and wants to keep some stuff in storage for a while.

There are companies that will go out and do a study of an area to find out what kind of need there is in any given area for different kinds of businesses. This is called a feasibility study company, and for a fee, they will do the study and tell you what the need in the area is for your service.

Chapter 5

Buying Condominiums to Rent Out with a Good Yield of Income versus Expenses

BUYING CONDOS TO RENT out for a profit requires a lot of investigation. You must find units with a high income versus expense ratio to make the maximum dollars from your investment. You will make a lot more money if you purchase a property for $15,000 that brings in $700 a month than to buy a $100,000 property that brings in $1,100 a month. You should be looking at a low-income type property to rent because the mark-up is a lot better.

I once purchased thirty condos for $30,000 per unit; those same condos are selling though tax sale certificate foreclosures for about $15,000 to $20,000 a unit now in bad times. Through short sales and foreclosures, you can purchase units very cheap these days. Let's run the numbers: a $15,000 unit will run you about $120,000 mortgage payments, $110 condo fees, $105.00 taxes. About $335 in fees and you're getting $700 for a month's rent. That's $365 a month profit per unit. That's what I call a good ratio.

I have a friend of mine who has two condos that were $130 each and he is only getting $775. A month, now he has a mortgage payment, condo fees and taxes to pay, but he is not making any money. If he would have bought in a market like today, he would be making a lot more money every month. Some people have

$300,000 homes that they are renting out for $1,600 a month. The numbers just weren't coming in at those prices.

You should be looking for fairly large corporations that got stuck with paying top dollar for condos and now are willing to take a loss and finance them for you to boot. Choose a corporation with twenty or thirty units who are willing to sell them cheap and make you a deal; now is the time.

There are many owners of these units that are trying desperately to get out. When you look at them, throw out a low ball offer, get them to hold financing to eliminate fees, offer them a low price and a low interest rate, get them to pay for settlement fees that when you're walking away from the deal, the worst they can say is no. Many people look at properties, hear the price, and walk away; they never make an offer, so they never get a deal. Another way to get many new deals is through tax sale certificate foreclosures, which we will go into in another chapter.

If you're going to look for these deals, you should try to sharpen your negotiating skills and be able to put a deal together once you sit down at the table. Go in with some comparisons of properties that have sold in the last years that compare with the properties you're buying. Bring up the fact that financing is hard to get and that there were a lot of foreclosures last year. Bring up other offers that were turned down, go in with your negotiations if you have to; it's better to have someone mad at you and get a good deal than to not get a good deal.

Find an out of the county condo owner that had bad management, are being foreclosed on, and are catching up on all the fees; make a deal with them for nothing down and rent them out with immediate income. Contact the condo associations and find out who is behind in their condo fees, and check with the township and see who is behind with their taxes, water, and sewer, and so on. Once you find out who owns them, contact them and offer to take them off the hook. You would be surprised what kind of deal you can make.

Remember, never sell anything that you ever buy; that's the secret of becoming wealthy. Every month of your life, you should do a new financial statement and keep track of your wealth so that it will always continue to grow.

Chapter 6

Building a Condominium Slip Marina Changing the Existing Marina into Highest and Best Use

FIND YOURSELF AN EXISTING run-down marina in a highly populated boaters' area. Go in and purchase the marina for about $15,000 a slip. Remember to get the property tied up to get approvals for condominium conversion. After you've got the marina tied up under contract, order your new floating docks; they should run about $4,000 each with new pilings and a six-foot drop in front of the marina to prevent the pasting boards from rocking the boats in the marina. You should be able to get a thousand dollars a foot selling out the slips. While you're getting your approvals, you're going to make sure you've got your buyers lined up and that there is a market for your product. If the market is not there, you will have a regular marina operation. Try to build a six-foot drop on the front T dock to prevent waves from the intercostal from rocking your boats that are parked in your marina.

Of course if you didn't sell out, once you got your approvals, you could sell some and rent the rest out. In order to get some investors involved, you have to be able to let your buyers also rent out the slips. To increase your profitability, you might want to put in a boat stacker to stack up the boats that are not in use all the time. You would have a forklift to drop the boats in when someone calls up and wants their boat in the water at a certain time. You would also get maximum use of the land like that. Try to build your boat ramp so you could accommodate both the forklift boats and the trailed-in boats. Build a repair garage on the property and rent it out to a boat machine. Try not to involve yourself in the day-to-day operation if you can help it so you have time for your other ventures.

If you can't find a rundown marina, you can always create one by finding a waterfront property that nobody can build on because it's in the wetlands. You would create a situation where you would build what is called a natural environment marina, one that can't be used for any other use but what you're using it for. You can, first of all, cross 1/3 of the water, depending on the area, to build your slips across the water. Then you put your pilings in, put in floating docks, and the idea is that everything is natural and you don't have any permanent structures on the property, such as buildings or a parking lot where the water can't drain through. So you would put up a tent material building until you're part of the community, then you can always go back and request a permit to build a building. Put in a patio that could afterward be a foundation for a building when you win everybody's favor in the township. Also a movable boat stacker and stones on the parking lot where water can flow without disturbing the land, so as to not have any environmental problems.

Usually, this type of property would have billboards on it and would be in the entrance to a seashore resort area, and you could lease the land cheap because it was between two billboards. As far as the township is concerned, you would be creating rateables for the township to make some more tax revenue out of the worthless wetlands. Wow, look at the location for boats; it's right on the way to the shore area with a cheap rent.

Another ideal for a marina would be to put in a floating home park to build beautiful homes on the water, next to the most expensive real estate around. Find a marina that is run-down on the outskirts of a resort town and build $150,000 to $300,000 homes floating in the water. First, you sell them the home and then you charge them to park the home there. Now the owners have a beautiful home on the water with their boat tied up next to the house next to a little floating dock that you can swim or fish off. Wow, that's nice.

Chapter 7

Buying a Shopping Center and Converting It to Condominium Stores to Make a Lot of Money

Go to the owner of a run-down and half-vacant shopping center and get him to give you the place till you can change it to the highest and best use. You need again the shopping center for a year to get the approvals so you will go into contract with the seller to make the change. After you go through the approval process of changing the shopping center to condominium stores and making them all fee simple; that is, separate deeds. You will approach the tenant that is paying $4,000 a month rent and sell him his store; now it's only going to cost him $2,900 a month. He's happy and you're wealthier; you should be able to make about $1.5 million converting a center to condos and selling it out to the tenants.

Getting tenants for the empty stores is simple too. Hire yourself a salesman to go to the other shopping centers in the area and approach the tenants and ask them if they want to expand their business and open another store like they have in your shopping center, and by the way, you can purchase your store; it's fee simple with its own deed and you can actually buy your store. If you want to pay rent forever, you can, but we're giving you an opportunity to buy your own. The stores that are for sale are always full as compared to the stores that pay rent. In our area, the stores have an 18 percent occupancy compared to the stores that are for rent and a 10 percent vacancy factor in the stores that are for sale. You can also co-op the units. The difference is you form a corporation, and if you have 100,000 square foot of stores, then each square foot owns one percent of the corporation. Now each tenant would pay condo fees, and you would own the condo association forever. In other words, if you had a 10,000 square foot store, you would own 10 percent of the corporation. This is another way to convert this shopping center. This is much less in legal fees to do it this way.

Use other people's credibility to finance and purchase these big deals. If you're just starting out on your million-dollar profit venture, you're going to need other people's credibility to proceed with these large deals. You're going to need someone who has the ability to borrow large sums of money and that has a lot of clout with banks and professional people to help you in your struggle to obtain these things that you need to start on your long journey to success. You have to decide what it is that you want to accomplish and go into it with unwavering courage and mastery of detail. First, you must find a large shopping center that's for sale, preferably ones that are in trouble; approach the owner, and ask him how much he wants for the center. Once he decides to sell it to you, then you must make your plan.

Contact someone who is big in processing and selling real estate for large profits, someone that for a fee, preferably a couple of hundred thousand dollars, would be willing to help you get started. You need this person's knowledge and credibility to get started because this is your first deal and you're going to have difficulty doing it yourself. Plan your deal so you'll make a million dollars on it, and plan to give a couple hundred thousand of that money to the person that's going to help you get that amount of money. You approach this new person and ask him to help you get a loan to borrow the money to purchase this large center; promise to pay him a nice sum if he is willing to help you. Ask him to introduce you to the lender and tell the lender that he is part of the deal. You will then go in and make your deal. Tell the seller of the center that you want to purchase the property from him. After he gives you the property, you start going through the approval process of getting it converted to condominium use, which will take about a year to accomplish.

After you got into agreements with the owner, you hire an architect to design the condominium separation design and start going through your approval process. Now all this time, you are speaking to the bank and telling them everything you're going to do so that when you're ready, they will give you the money to purchase the center and they will be able to handle the end loans after you purchase the center and sell it out to the present and future tenants-owners of the condos. The whole idea here is to purchase the center for one price and to convert the stores to condos and then sell them to the present tenants; you approach the guy who is paying $4,000.

Chapter 8

How to Control Millions of Dollars' Worth of Real Estate without Actually Purchasing It

A FRIEND OF MINE purchased a shopping center for $1.2 million a few years ago, where he put up a $5,000 deposit and put it in agreements. The center was very large and worth about three million. Forty-five days after, he put the deal into agreements. He sold it for $2.4 million dollars to a bank, and the bank flipped it to a Mormon group for $2.8 million the same day. I remember that day; we had three settlements for the same title company on the same day. I remember the bank that was financing the center wanted a master lease done because the owner of the center was renting it to himself at $3 a foot and the bank wanted it rented for $6 before they would make the loan. So my friend had to do a master lease for five years for $6 a foot because it was a five-year loan. The thing about this deal was my friend actually tied up the property for forty-five days, giving him time to settle it with a third party.

You don't have to purchase a property to be able to sell it or flip it. All you have to do is to go into agreements of sale and do everything in that agreement that it says to do and you will control that deal until it's finished. The wording would be as such, Robert Domico, or assignee, or nominee, or New Jersey Corporation to be formed, hereafter known as buyer. At this point, as long as the seller accepts the agreement and signs it, you have complete control over that real estate, as long as you do whatever the agreement says, even if the real estate is worth ten million dollars.

At this point, you can do whatever you wish with the agreement. You can syndicate it, you can sell it to someone else by doing an assignment agreement, you can flip it, or you can lease purchase it if you decide to buy it yourself after you don't get your financing. If you don't get the financing, you can get the seller to hold a mortgage, once he has it in his mind that the place is sold. You can tell the seller that if he gets cash, he will have to pay capital gain taxes, but if he holds a mortgage, he can pay it in installment taxes, paying the taxes over time, not all at once. Once the seller signs the paper, you have complete control over that piece of real estate until the contract expires. Make sure you put a clause in the contract that says if for any reason this does not settle in sixty days, there will be a thirty-day extension.

Now that you know how to control millions of dollars' worth of real estate, you should make it your life's work to put as many deals in contract as you can. As soon as you sell one, you hit a homerun, and you can do some of the other deals in my book. Still, you don't need money to do some other deals in the book. Another friend of mine had a four-hundred-unit apartment building, he put in agreements for four million dollars. The guy that bought it realized that it was worth six million dollars; he put it on the market for $5.5 million and sold it in thirty days. My friend, after he put it in agreements, realized that it was really worth much more than he put it in agreements for and called me.

He said, "Bob, how do I get out of these agreements? I signed them."

My response unfortunately was "There is nothing you can do at this point because you already signed the agreements."

The guy, without even going to settlement, assigned the agreements to another buyer and made $1.5 million.

It is easy to control millions of dollars of real estate by just putting the deal into agreements of sale, if you can convince the guy to put it in agreements and promising a deposit down the road. Once you convince investors to put up the deposit money, you can go into agreements. Find someone who has a structured settlement, someone who hit the lottery, someone who recently got an inheritance, and advertise this on Craigslist or other free websites. Once you get this big deal into agreements, get a list of everyone within a fifteen-mile radius that make $300,000 a year and show them the tax advantages of investing with you. You will send them direct mail, telling them about your project. You are going to form a syndication to raise any money that you may need. Even if this book is about purchasing large parcels of real estate with no money, it stands to reason that you can make more money quicker if you have a lot of money to invest. Remember, this book is about using other people's credibility and other people's money to make money for you.

For example, using other people's clients by offering a small piece of the deal to accountants, lawyers, bank managers, or anybody who has control over people's investments or financial decisions. You can get these clients because they respect the decisions of people that have degrees in certain types of business who give people advice what they should invest in. These ideals are very important, and as you go through my book, you should remember these simple rules. Getting back to controlling large parcels of real estate by putting them into agreements, it is possible to have a portfolio of many deals in agreements once you establish a system for putting deals to gather with no deposits. You must be able to convince the seller that you are going to take his property and put it in to a higher and better use and make it worth more money. If you're not successful in your quest, you will give the unfinished performance back to the seller so that he can continue the process once you give him the idea. For example, say you are buying a lot to build a shopping center on it, and you convince him to go into agreements with you and then get the deal started with the engineers and other professional people that you need for double their normal fees.

If you don't complete the deal, you will give it back to the seller, and he can finish the deal, which will be much more valuable when he gets it back. For example, if you hire an engineer on a contingency for double his normal fee to get the shopping center approved for you and he is successful in getting his approvals, then you will put these approvals on the seller's desk after you've made the land twice more valuable by getting preliminary approvals for them. By promising to do this, you get the seller to go into agreements with you with no deposit. Remember, once you go into agreements with the seller, you have total control over the real estate deal; once again, after you get the seller's signature on that agreement and you control this million-dollar profit deal, which the seller can't get out of.

Once you get proficient in putting these deals in agreements, then the world is yours. Remember you're going after people who have owned the property for years and never developed it. I once went into agreements with a guy to build an eighty thousand square foot mini storage complex. After I got the deal approved, I found a buyer to purchase the project, land, and approvals for $750,000; I was in agreements for $500,000. I only made the contact for one year; after it took me a year to get it approved, the seller decided to take the land back. The buyers with whom I was selling it to made contact with the guy I was purchasing the property from; he sold my buyer the property for $750,000 instead of getting $500,000, which I was in contact with him for. So never put short time units on any deal; remember, it's going to take you at least a year to get it approved, so give yourself two years if you can.

I believe the long-time property owner slowed up the approval process deliberately so that my time would run out. Beware of greedy property owners; don't put forth an effort like I did and lose time like that. I guess I can't complain. I had a lot of good deals in my life. The timing was bad; we went into a recession right after that and the place never got built anyway.

After that, I went into a deal where I found a large piece of unbuildable wetlands right outside the Atlantic City between two billboards owned by the billboard company. The highest and best use for this land was to build a marina. The sellers had no idea want to do with the property, which was backed up to a waterway that was deep enough to launch boats. I covered the land with large stones so that the rain would fall through and big-enough stones that wouldn't get caught in small tires, the type that boat trailers have on them. Once I opened the marina and everybody got used to what it was, I applied for a variance to put a boat stacker on the property. Then I purchased a forklift and stacked up another one hundred boats on the property. The boats' owners would call up and say, "I'll be at the marina at three p.m." We sold the business for many times as much as we had into it.

Chapter 9

The Master of Mirrors

My clients in New York who I did a lot of business with over the years tagged me with the name Master of Mirrors because I was able to put a deal together when no one else could. When I didn't have the wherewithal to do the big deals, I would use other people's credibility, credit, and knowledge to help me with deals and where needed. I would contact a person who was making millions of dollars in real estate and ask him to help me with the financing and introduce me to some of the people that he deals with, and I would cut him in on the deal, so he could make a few bucks out of the deal. I would maybe use some of his credit to get the loan and some of his experience in putting the deal together.

If I was syndicating the deal, I would call accountants and attorneys to try and get some of their investors to get into some of my deals, using the credibility of the professionals who represent them. Again, I would give the professionals a small percentage of the deal for coming in and jumping on the running train. I would go in and get the property approved for whatever I wanted to do with it and then run the numbers, show income and expenses, draw the concepts, package the deal, make it appetizing to the group, and get them interested. I would also get a list of everybody within a thirty-mile radius who made over $300,000 a year and contact all the people who hit the lottery, got an inheritance, or just got a structured settlement. I would sit down with these people who had the money to invest and try to put the deal together.

This is what the investors called putting a deal together with mirrors.

The guys from New York were a group that I had sold a warehouse to that was in bankruptcy. Several years before, it was formally a meat company; it was 240,000 square feet, and they filled it with soy beans until the market went bad and they stopped importing them, then they had an empty warehouse all of a sudden. So I decided to sell them tax sale certificates; they got a few properties out of that, but they didn't do that great with them either as it turned out, mostly because it wasn't their line of work.

Soon after that, I sold them two condo projects in Florida that the bank had repossessed from people who purchased them to convert them from apartment units to condos. They were unsuccessful because they didn't have a plan when they went into the deal. Whenever you go into any deal, you should have an alternate plan to convert to if the plan doesn't work, you would change to something else. For example, if you start to convert apartments to condominiums and you're not selling them out fast enough, rent them out or offer them for time-share if it's in a resort area, as it's always better to be in a resort area to have these other options.

Anyway, I sold them condo conversions that the bank in Florida had taken back, foreclosed on. One was sixty units that were made to sell for $250,000 each and didn't sell out fast enough to carry the large mortgage that they had on them. So my guys in New York purchased them and rented them out for a while until the real estate market got better. If you could, for some reason, rent them out, then you have to call the welfare department and rent them out to section 8; what you really don't want to do unless you have to.

There's always an alternative rather than to lose the units back to the bank. If the unemployment rate goes up and more people get out of work, then the section 8 market gets better. You can always go back and redo the units when the good market comes back down the road. Remember in the first chapter, I said never sell any real estate that you ever buy for your whole life and you will become very rich.

You have to move with the flow of the economy. Think before you do anything and go with the flow, rather than to proceed with an idea that you have before you go into that particular job that you're trying to do. There are many things you can do with an apartment building, specifically apartments, condo conversion, co-op, welfare rentals, time-shares, or you can convert part of the building into offices, etc.

The differences in these options are as follows:

1. To make it into condos: Go to the township and tell them you want to convert the apartments into condos. You will hire an architect to draw up the changes and an engineer to make the changes. It will probably cost you about $50,000 to convert one hundred units. Of course, the advantage is that you can sell the now fee-simple units to individuals because they all have separate deeds, like single-family homes have. The cinder block walls of a condo would have to be raised right to the roof to keep the next condo from catching on fire in case there was a fire.

2. Co-op conversion would be a conversion like this: you would form a corporation. If you have a hundred units, each member of the corporation would own 1 percent of the corporation, then you would form a condo association, and each owner-member would pay condo fees to take care of the expenses for the building, property taxes, insurance, trash removal, and common-area repair expenses. The repairs that are to be done within the walls of your unit would be paid by the owner of the unit. This would be the most inexpensive way to convert the complex.

3. Time-share is usually done in resort areas for vacationers who are only going to be there for a short time's stay. You would rent the units for a short time stay for a large amount of money, for example, a thousand dollars a week. The time-share is the highest yield of income you could possibly make out of an apartment complex other than a hotel condominium, which deals with smaller units usually, which we will go into also.

If you find you are losing the property back to the bank, take out a second mortgage to make payments on the first mortgage, but whatever you do, don't let the property go; keep it till you decide what you're going to do with it.

The hotel condominium is the highest and best use you could ever make of a building, except for time-share, because you are selling the condo units for a good price and running a hotel business afterward, renting the rooms on a daily basis and charging the owners 25 percent of the room rental on a daily basis. The buyers of the condo units because it's in the passive income bracket gets about a $37,000 write-off each year because he can write off the vacancy factor, the electric gas, the 25 percent the owner of the condo association charges you, etc. The units will sell out in about six months because of the write-offs. Time-share is a little bit better because you are selling units for about $10,000 a week, meaning that the time-share owner buys one week a year use for $10,000, one unit sells for $500,000.

You must buy this hotel in a resort area to be able to sell the time-shares out to vacationers. A place like Atlantic City where you have the seashore for the summer season and gambling for the rest of the year would be a better location for the hotel condominium or a time-share.

If you're interested in a location in Atlantic City, call the author of this book.

Chapter 10

Putting a Billboard Company Together from Scratch and Making Money off the Rest of the Land

THE MOST VALUABLE PART of the land is the frontage because the frontage is already improved where the rest of the land is not. For example, if you find a farm that is for sale and you would like to take it to highest and best use, you would approach the owner and tell him you want to take his farm to highest and best use and you will get the land approved at your expense. The land on the front is already improved because you don't have to put roads in to get to it, so the rest of the land is approved even if only the frontage is improved.

A property with three road frontages is the most valuable of all because it's got more linear footage of improved land on it. Making the land more valuable by getting approvals on it is making millions of dollars without building anything on it. We will be into getting land approved and selling to developers in a later chapter. If you have to two miles of frontage, then you have two miles of improved land which you can immediately build on because it's right on the road frontage. Because once again, the land is already improved, you don't have to get it approved because it's already got a road in front of it. So if you find a farm with one and a half miles of road frontage, you can build right away because you don't have to put a road to get to it.

Now let's say that you purchase this farm, say one hundred acres, and you can build thirty houses on the front of the land without any roads in, or let's say, you don't build the houses at all; you just sell off the front lots for $40,000 each. Let's say you paid $500,000 or $5,000 an acre for the land, and you sold the thirty lots in the front for $40,000 each; that's $1.2 million, that's $700,000 profit without building anything. Wow.

Now you put an easement in to get to the rest of the property, put roads in to build the rest of the property out, or get another 20 percent for roads, so you get another fifty-six houses or lots inside the property. If you sell the rest of the lots off for $40,000 each, that's another $2,240 profit; now you made $3,240 just by subdividing and selling off the lots.

Pay the $500,000 that you paid for the farm and you got a nice profit of $2.74, minus the cost of putting the roads in, say another $45,000, still leaves over $2.6 million profit on the property. If you have a lot of extra frontage, you might want to put a billboard on the beginning and on the other end of the property for extra income. It's always good to be in the billboard business while you're investing in other ventures. The potential is also there for other types of uses; pick up a zoning map when you go in to the township, select some land for other uses, such as self-storage if the area has a lot of houses with no basements, or maybe they need a shopping center or an over-fifty-five community. They love them because the owners pay taxes, but they don't have any kids in school; that's a gravy train for a township. See if the township is in need of an industrial park, a trailer park, or whatever they are looking at for somebody to build; it's a lot easier to get approval to build if you're building what they need.

Chapter 11

Buying Something and Making It Worth Much More by Doing Several Things to It

REMEMBER RULE NUMBER 1 whenever you are building something: build what they need, not what they already have enough of. You can also be in the business of finding out what they need, buying the land, getting it approved for that purpose, and selling it to a developer; that's always a good business to be in. First, run demographics and see that they have the population to support a property of a certain type. Always go into an area that is expanding in a certain direction and get in front of the expansion or block the expansion with more development. Maybe the town needs a marina, a camp ground, an industrial park, whatever.

It is also good to buy a large piece of land that is landlocked and purchase an easement to get into it and make the land more valuable. I had a friend of mine who bought one thousand acres of land on Route 295 south in New Jersey for $500 an acre and then sold the land to a developer for $3.2 million. You can create great value in any real estate deal by improving the land, by converting it to highest and best use, or changing the zoning on it, or creating access to it.

Find an old warehouse on the riverfront on about five acres, knock down the warehouse, go in and get the approvals for a condominium development with boat slips; each unit gets a free boat slip. Either your buyers are into boating or they rent the slip out for additional income and sell them out or market a group of people that are into boating or make it a retirement community that consist of boating people, many people over fifty-five have boats too. Make it an over-fifty-five community that consists of boaters. The township would love you; they don't have any kids in school, but they still pay property taxes. Wow, easy approvals there.

You can make a piece of land much more valuable by changing the use. For example, buying a house next to a business and going in to the township and asking them to change the house to commercial use; make sure you put in the contract when you are purchasing it, contingent on getting approvals for commercial use in the contract, so you can get out of the deal if you don't get the new zoning. After you get the zoning, the owner can't take it back and try to get the zoning himself because you just doubled the value of the property; instead of renting the house for $1,000 a month, you can rent it out for $14 a foot a year. Using a 10 percent capitalization rate, which we'll get into in another chapter, the house is worth double what you paid for it.

The zonings start with residential, then go to professional, then to commercial, then to industrial. The reason for that is nobody opens a body shop next to a residence. Also higher uses such as strip clubs and pornographic establishments and couples clubs are very valuable zonings to the right people. Remember, if you can change the zoning to a higher and better use, you're going to make a lot of money when you sell it or rent it out. There is a lot of money in putting deals in contract, contingent upon changing the use and then assigning the contract to another buyer with an assignment agreement, which will get into in another chapter.

Whenever you can, take something that has value and convert to something that has more value; you are finding the highest and best use for the property, thus making much more valuable and profitable when you sell it. It makes sense in converting something to a higher and better use to increase the value of a piece of property. For example, find a large warehouse, maybe two hundred or even three hundred square feet; find it on a highway with 200,000 cars a day going by. The busier the highway, the better the deal; you want a couple hundred cars a day looking at your site to get maximum exposure, with many cars going by and looking down on your site. You're looking a site that has a closed-down warehouse on it that's at least on about maybe five to seven acres so you can really sink your teeth into this site with a great deal. Now you have this two hundred sq. ft. plus warehouse, how are you going to make it valuable? Well, first you are going to approach the owner and tell him that you would like to buy his warehouse.

You would like to take the property and bring it to its highest and best use; be sure you don't tell the owner what the highest and best use is or he will do it himself and take your idea and run with it, leaving you high and dry. You then convince him to put the deal into agreement with you so you can then run with your idea. Remember once you've got a deal in agreements signed and sealed, you have total control over the deal. Once he signs that contract and you do everything that that contract says you have total control over it. Now you go out and hire an engineer to go into the township and change the use of this warehouse that right now is a big eyesore with over two thousand cars a day looking at it and seeing how much of an eyesore it really is. So the city would like it improved so it doesn't look so bad. First, you are going to gingerbread the side of the building that's facing the highway so it looks better, and you're going to bring drawings into city hall and show them how nice it's going to look when it's finished, once you get them to consider the use that you're trying to get, you tell them what you wish to do with that big eyesore.

You will then go in with drawings of what you're going to do with it and what its use will be. The use will be a self-storage complex with a couple hundred feet of self-storage. You will go in and build 10×10 and 10×20 foot cages inside and put a big sign on it that 200,000 cars a day will see and call it cheap self-storage. You will actually take a warehouse that was getting $4 a foot for warehouse space and change it into $25 a foot warehouse space, making the property worth at least six times as much as you paid for it when it is finished and rented out. For example, if you paid $250 for the warehouse, using a 10 percent capitalization rate, you get about $1.8 million after it's all built and fully rented out. Now imagine 200,000 cars a day looking at a sign on the roof that says Cheap Self-Storage Syndication, $50,000 minimum investment, and raise half a million so you have no trouble putting this deal together.

Now, let's see how much you will make on this deal. If you paid $250,000 for a property and you build, take off 20 percent for hallways, say 160,000 square feet of space at $25 a foot a year, that's an income of $400,000 a year using a 10 percent capitalization rate that makes the property worth $4,000,000; that's my idea of highest and best use.

Chapter 12

Building a Trailer Park Is Relatively Easy If You Have the Zoning

FIND A PIECE OF land in a relatively highly populated area, about ten acres with access from the main road. Go into the township with your attorney to set a meeting and try to find out if you can build a trailer park in their township. It is important to bring some renderings in and give them an idea what the place is going to look like, the layout and the way the trailers will be positioned, and the amount of recreation you will have: pool, playground, clubhouse, whatever you intend to do to make it a desirable contribution to the community.

The township will probably take a while to give you an okay so don't get impatient with them; wait it out and try to win their favor by letting them know that you're a nice person and you will work with them. Tell them that you will have a committee to represent the owners of the trailers, that you will have monthly meetings to protect the trailer owners, and that you will run the operation like a small community and not necessarily like a trailer park. Let them know how you are going to set it up: selling the lots or just renting the lots, will it be a co-op ownership, a single-family type operation or a fee-simple type operation. Once you get the approvals, you can go into contract to purchase the land. Hopefully when you decided to build this park, you went into agreements contingent on getting approvals and didn't go in and just purchased the land without knowing whether you could build a park on it or not. After you get the zoning approved, you will start getting the approvals to build and start building the development.

Maybe you want to tell the township that you sell trailers for a certain company and get approvals to have a distributorship to sell trailers on the property while you're at it. Then you're going to hire an engineer to design your park for you, the size of the lots, the distance between the lots, and so on. You must decide what type of park you wish to have: is it an over fifty-five community or a single-family development with a playground and if you're selling the lots out or you're going to rent them or maybe both. You start to build your park and do some pre-advertising to create some pre-sales so you have some more money to finish your project with. Usually, you start your advertising the minute you get your approvals so that you have some deposits. Remember, the more deposits you have, the easier it is to get your financing approved.

Now that your park is under construction, you're going to start having open houses for your simple trailer that you have on display and take more orders for other trailers that you can now sell. It's nice for people to bring their own trailers in, but it's better if you sell them one yourself.

You have to decide whether you want to sell the lots, rent or sell the trailers, or all of the above. No matter what you do, you are going to make a lot of money. If you have a problem financing the park, there are several ways you can do it: (1) get an SBA loan from the government, (2) get an EDA loan from the state, (3) get a conventional loan from a bank, or (4) you can always syndicate the deal by taking in partners. If you do a limited partnership and you become the general partner, you can still be in charge and make all the decisions or you can get into agreements for control. You can make a deal with the contractor to pay for the work on a piecemeal contract and pay for the construction as it sells, or it leases out, or however you are going to make money from the park you share it with the contractor. On the sales part, it's easy to sell a lot and pay for it on an installment kind of payment.

Chapter 13

Building a Water Home Park, Selling the Homes, Renting the Homes, Selling Out the Spaces, Renting Out the Spaces, or All of the Above

FIND AN OLD MARINA or a piece of waterfront property, preferably near a resort area where people would want to stay in their water homes in the summertime. After you get the land in agreements with all the contingencies to get whatever it is your trying to accomplish approved, you will subdivide the marina into large-enough slips to put large-sized floating homes in; they would sell for between $150,000 and $250,000 each. Each party would have a large slip to put their home in, plus be able to tie a small boat up to the floating home.

Then you would put a pool in and maybe a small clubhouse, depending on the size of the marina, about five acres would be nice. Because they are floating homes, you would hook up gas, electricity, water, sewer, and cable TV. There are very few types of floating home parks in the United States, so it should be fairly easy to get zoning, mainly because there are not a lot of parks to compare it to. A town has to get comparisons to use while pricing the amount of taxes to charge and the type of zoning, then they can come up with one to fit your needs.

You can sell floating homes, you could sell houseboats, you could sell all marina-type products, and even put boats for sale on consignments. It is possible with this type of business to make a lot of money. After you get all that work done, you might even get zoning for a waterfront development down the line, maybe condos or high-end over-fifty-five communities with boat slips. You would try to get a split zoning commercial and residential, so you could perform a split use. A floating house park can get a few more dollars for everything they do because they are in a resort area.

You might be able to put a boat stacker on the property and have a launching area, where someone could call up and want their boat put in the water at a certain time, and you would go to the boat stacker with a forklift and take their boat down and put it in the water at a certain time, when they get back, put their boat back on the boat stacker. There are many services you could perform, I am just mentioning a few.

You could purchase a dealership and sell a certain type of boat, like popular family sporting boat or maybe a certain type of fishing boat, something in demand with a good market to bring in more revenue. You might put in a small clam bar or a fishing tackle store that sells bait, have a boat ramp and charge a fee for launching small boats, the potential is endless. Remember whatever you do, try to actualize the potential to get the most out of it and that you are making the investment the best that it can be.

You should be able to build your slips in the water about 40 percent across the water from your land to the other side; take advantage of the waterway laws and get the most of what you're doing by putting in those extra slips to improve your income. Winter storage in the water should also be available for those that don't find it necessary to put out their house boats every year; it's costly and the boat bottoms with multi-season paint are not required to be pulled out every year. This is another way to increase your income by charging additional in water rental for the wintertime. Winterizing will keep a full-time mechanic busy twelve months out of the year, cleaning, and waxing them, and detailing them out, when they get ready to put in the water. With all the various ways to make income from this good business, it makes it a good investment.

Chapter 14

Purchasing Land, Getting It Approved, and Selling It to a Developer

YOU PURCHASE A FEW acres of land in an area that is in the path of development where everything is moving and other developers are building, in an area where functional obsolescence does not exist. Once you find this fast-moving developing area, you run a feasibility study and see what the area is in need of.

Say the area needs a large shopping center. You would approach the owner of the land and tell him that you would like to purchase his land to see if you can put a large shopping center on it. You will need the land for a year to see if the township and the city fathers will allow such a development in their town. Nobody buys anything unless they can do what they want with it. The owner of the property has to give you the property for a year so that you can get the approvals to build your project. If for some reason you don't buy the property after a year, then you will put on his desk every approval you get on the piece of land.

You then go out and hire an engineer to see if it is feasible to build a center; he will go into the town and proceed to get the building approvals. First, you have to test the ground to see if it works by doing borings and then you show setbacks and find out how many square feet you can build on the property.

After you achieve this, you will want an architect to design a building for you that will fit the engineer's specifications and then draw the building and do the renderings of what it looks like. Say you build a 250,000 square foot shopping center and you get the project approved through the township. Now you're ready to contact large chain stores, get a large anchor store and a sub-anchor, and maybe some other famous name stores to come in. The more commitments you have, the easier it is to get financing and approvals. Once you get a commitment from a large anchor store or two, you can package your deal like such.

Take the renderings from the architect and make that the front of your package with a breakdown of the square footage of each unit and information about your new tenants. Then have an accountant do a projected income of what the property's income will be, what the projected taxes and expenses will be, and what the profit will be to the developer who buys the property. You see, the property has four values: one is the value of the land, two is the value of the approved site, three is the value with the building on it, and four is the value after its rented out and fully occupied.

You could sell this property for four different amounts of money depending when you sold it. At a point that you would sell it after it was built and rented out, you would then sell it to an investor. Getting land approved is the most money you will ever make out of a real estate deal. Start today and put a deal together. It's as easy as getting an option on a piece of land, with contingency to put whatever it is that you have in mind together and make it work; the rest is up to you, so go for it. Move forward with unwavering courage and mastery of detail.

Chapter 15

Pulling Money out of Real Estate by Refinancing

You purchase a building for $550,000; you get it appraised for $1,000,000. You borrow 80 percent loan to value, you put down $220,000, then you go out and refinance it for the appraised value of $1,000,000, and they will give you 80 percent loan to value, so you just made $330,000 in your pocket; that's the theory. As long as the income from the property is enough to pay the monthly mortgage payment on the property, you can do this all day long and create a vast amount of money and a large credit line to top it off.

There are many ways to pull money out of real estate. Another way is by purchasing the property and changing it to a higher and better use; we will talk a lot about highest and best use in this book. An example would be to purchase a building rented out as a warehouse, bringing in $600 a square foot and year, and converting into an office building and now bringing $15 a foot a year. After it's rented out, you can pull out at least double what you paid for the building.

Remember, you're never going to sell anything that you purchase so the income will definitely pay for the mortgage and render you a nice profit each and every month. Just remember to invest that money that you make on capital gains into a building of greater value, so you don't have to pay taxes on the gain. In today's market, there are a lot of good real estate deals out there that are just waiting for someone to come along and purchase them and usually at a good price. Look for a business that is in bankruptcy; go to the US bankruptcy court in your area and go through the files. Find a great deal that you can purchase for a good price and decide what you're going to do with it before you purchase it.

When you find a good deal, study the area by performing a feasibility study to see what the area needs and who is going to support it. Check the population and how many people will use whatever service you will render, and make sure there is a need for whatever you decide to do with the building. After you decide what it is you're going to do with the building, move forward and proceed; remember, time is money. After you build whatever it is that you are going to build, create an income that you can get a 10 percent cap rate from and then refinance to get ready to pull out your money. You are going to have to hire an engineer and an architect to make the change to that higher and better use that you are trying to accomplish, to create a higher income from the property.

Once you make the change, then you have to rent it out or do what you have to do to make the change.

Chapter 16

The Master of Mirrors Is the Master of Syndications

My investors up in New York tagged me with the name Master of Mirrors for my ability to put together large deals for them.

When I came out of the service years ago at age twenty-one, I put syndications together on three delicatessens. In those days, you could get the meat companies to give you a meat case, the ice cream companies to give you an ice cream case and a frozen food case free. The roll company would build you counters with built-in roll bins on the front of the counters, and the grocery companies would build you shelves. The only things you had to buy were two slicers, two scales, two cash registers, and a sign out front, and you were in business. For about $5,000, you opened a deli. Anyway, I got two other guys to put up $5,000 each, and we opened three delis.

I sold the delis after three years and for $60,000, a net profit of $45,000 plus all the income we made. After that I opened Paulsboro Cafeteria in Paulsboro, New Jersey, with another three guys. It cost us about $45,000 with all used equipment, and we sold it for $150,000 in about eighteen months.

I then put a small group together and opened Louisiana Seafood House in Alexandria, Virginia. It was like a Red Lobster, a regular seafood menu with ten items that were all-you-could-eat. We worked with the place for about a year, then opened another place call Domico's Seafood House in North Beach, Maryland, thirty-five miles away. We sold both places in another eighteen months for three times as much as they cost us.

Then I moved back to New Jersey. I formed another syndication on a place called Lucien's Old Tavern in Berlin, New Jersey, with five guys. While I still had ownership in Lucien's, I put another place together called Schrul's in McKee City, New Jersey, with a different five guys. Both Lucien's and Schrul's were more than seventy years old. I was going to franchise them both but never did. While I still had ownership of the two places, I opened Executive Inn Banquets at the Holiday Inn in Vineland, New Jersey, with only one partner.

When I started doing syndications, I used to form general partnerships, where everybody was responsible for everything: property taxes, state and government taxes, with everybody at risk. But afterward, I decided to do limited partnerships, where only the general partner was at risk and the most that doctors, lawyers, or Indian chefs could lose was what they put into the deal. The way I put a deal together was that the general partner would run the operation and have all the responsibility, mostly because he was salaried and no one else was, and the investors got their percentage of the profit.

At first, I syndicated mostly because of restaurants as I was raised in the restaurant business and knew it so well. Later on, I started syndications on self-storage complexes, first building them and then converting existing warehouses into self-storage places. If I found a warehouse that was bringing in $6 a foot a year, I would build little cages of 10×10 and 10×20 inside and get $25 a foot a year, increasing the value of the property by five or six times. Then, because I was a boater most of my life, I decided to purchase a couple of boats and sell them as a time-share. I figured with all the hurricanes going on, I could buy a boat for pennies on a dollar, restore it, and then sell the boat as time-share for $10,000 a week or maybe invest $100,000 in a boat and make $500,000 selling it for time-share.

First I bought a fifty-four-foot hunter sailing yacht from Katrina, restored it to almost brand-new, and sold it time-share for $10,000 per week in Florida. Then I bought a fifty-two-foot trawler from another hurricane in Florida and took it over on the Chesapeake Bay, then sold that for $10,000 a week time-share. The trawler had two- to four-cylinder engines in it and was much easier to operate than a sailboat, which had to be captained each time it was taken out. But instead of buying a half million-dollar boat that they are only going to use a few weeks a year, spend $10,000 for one week or $20,000 for two weeks a year and get the same buzz.

When you do a syndication, you have to have a plan. All of the syndications I put together had a plan. I would take a motel in a resort area and convert it to hotel condominiums, maybe pay $25,000 per room and convert them into hotel condominiums and sell them converted for $150,000 per room as hotel condominiums; they sold out fast because they were passive income instead of ordinary income. I would buy a shopping center and convert it into condominium stores, maybe go to the guy who is paying $4,000 a month rent for a store and tell him if he buys the store it is only going to cost him $2,900 a month; you should make about $1.5 million on a 150,000 square foot shopping center. You can syndicate anything you want as long as it makes money. If you list a restaurant that makes a million a year profit, everybody and his brother will want to put a hundred thousand in it because they are going to get back $75,000 to $80,000 every year. What a retirement plan that is.

Let's run the numbers. Pick an Italian restaurant that is doing for example $3.5 million a year. Say you convince the seller to sell it for two million dollars. If the restaurant has a large wine inventory and has an excellent wine sale content going every month, where the top wine sales server gets a nice size bonus every month, enough to make them compete for it. Say the wine sales go up to 30 percent and then the place could easily do 30 percent total profit for the year. Now if the seller will take one million down on this $3.3 million dollar a year at 30 percent profit, you would make over a million a year; it would be considered for franchising if it makes that kind of profit at that point, which is a whole other deal.

If whoever puts in a $100,000 could get $75,000 to $80,000 a year back for conceivably the rest of your life, that's a great retirement plan. How hard would it be to syndicate this restaurant? Easy, right. You should be able to put the group together in about a month. Say you're a real estate broker and you have $200,000 in commission coming and you decide to put the money back in the deal as one of the investors. You would own 20 percent of the restaurant and get $150,000 to $160,000 a year for the rest of your life.

I had a habit all my life of putting money (commissions) back to my deals and getting ownership in many businesses or in many cases. If I made $100,000 commission on a liquor store or a carwash, I would lend the commission back to the buyer and collect interest for about five years if the buyer didn't have all the money to put down; it made the deal work. Being an unlicensed business broker, I am able to put commissions back to deals. I am able to pay a finder's fee to lawyers, accountants, or any other professional that I see fit to get their clients. Being under the rule of the real estate commission, you have a whole other set of rules that you have to follow, and you're not able to do what I do.

Chapter 17

Syndicating a Co-Op Situation for a Large Profit

You find a large property with two hundred or three hundred units that's kind of run-down and needs revamping in a decent neighborhood, one that's maybe in the path of development, and not in a neighborhood that's functionally obsolete. Go to the owner and tell him you want to purchase his property and take it to the highest and best use, but don't tell him what you're going to do with it; he might decide to do it himself. Go into agreements, contingent on getting the highest and best use out of the property, which might take a year to get approved, so he has to give you the property for a year so you can change it into highest and best use, and at this point, you don't know what that is yet, you tell the owner.

Remember that you can control any piece of property no matter how expensive it is once you put it into agreements, as long as you do everything that the agreement of sale says from the day he signs it to you to control it. Now that you are controlling this large piece of real estate, what are you going to do with it? It will be necessary as you get these approvals to put copies of everything that you do on the seller's desk as you move along because if you wind up not buying it, then at least you leave the seller with some approvals so he can finish getting it approved and make something out of the deal; that's the least you can do for wasting the man's time.

Now, remember when you have anything in agreements, you totally control it. That means you can assign the agreements to someone else. With an assignment agreement, for a quick profit, you can syndicate it, or you can do what you originally planned to do, and get it approved for your highest and best use. You will now move forward with your plans to make the property more valuable. You will go out and get yourself an engineer, an architect, a lawyer, and an accountant to handle your conversion package for you. The best way to proceed on a move like this is to get them to do it on a contingency basis where you will pay them double their ordinary fees if they wait till after it sells to a developer or whatever you're going to do with it. If you decide at this point you want to continue and do the deal yourself, you can. Have the engineer start the work on converting the complex, from apartments to co-op units, going through the fire codes and so on. The architect will go to the township and change any required to change from apartments to co-op, and the lawyer will represent the group at the township hearing as they are scheduled. The accountant will do projected performances, showing what the income will be for the investors to review.

You then will proceed with the conversion to co-ops. You will form a corporation with three hundred shares so that the ownership of the co-op will be owned equally by the occupants of the three hundred units. In other words, each occupant will own a one-third share in the corporation that owns the complex. The owners will pay whatever the price is to buy the co-op unit. The group can make a healthy profit converting an apartment to co-op.

Chapter 18

Make Money in Real Estate by Opening a Business Brokerage

I STARTED MANY YEARS ago owning a lot of business by selling them and putting my commission back in the deals and owning whatever share of the business that I put up. In other words, if the business was $100,000, I would put up the $10,000 commission, if the buyer put up $50,000, then I would own 20 percent of the business. Of course, I would always be a silent partner and get 20 percent at the end of the year. The guy that owned the other 80 percent would get 80 percent of the profit and a salary for running the place that was decided by both of us in the beginning. I started in the business in 1978, and at one time, I owned part of twenty-five businesses. My income from this brought me a nice salary for a lot of years. You can open a business brokerage. In most states, you don't even need a license of any kind, except for the states like Florida, where they say to draw up a lease, you need a real estate license. But in Delaware, New Jersey, and Pennsylvania, where I mostly operated, you didn't need one.

The first syndication I put together was a very large restaurant, with six guys who each put up cash to come into the deal. Once again, whatever they put up was the percentage that they owned of the business. The business sold for $1.2 million and we got in for $240,000 down. I put my commission of $120,000 back in and owned 50 percent of the whole deal. It was my first big deal; I thought I was ruling the whole world in those days. The idea certainly will work, and it's a way to own many business and be able to make a lot of money without putting up any of your own cash. Once you get the place listed for sale under contract, you more or less control the whole deal. Put an ad in the paper, "Syndication large landmark restaurant, five people with $400,000 each to own 20 percent of large restaurant. Bring your friends and business associates to your restaurant for dinner, have your wife's birthday party there, and your daughter's wedding, you will probably spend $40,000 on your daughter's wedding anyway." So the restaurant makes $200,000 a year, so you put in $120,000 of someone else's money to get $100,000 a year back, not bad at all. We did a general partnership, which was a big mistake, so the next one I did was a limited partnership with a general partner who was responsible for all the liabilities, US taxes, property taxes, unemployment, social security, state taxes, and whatever the other liabilities were. The investors were doctors, lawyers, and Indian chefs, and they were not responsible for their investments, so the most they could lose is what they put into the deals, but they got all the write-offs, five years' depreciation on equipment and fixtures, thirty years' level depreciation on real estate, etc.

Over the years, there were many businesses I owned part of, but I always insisted on a daily budget report from each one. The insurance bill divided by 365, the electric bill divided by thirty, the property taxes bill divided by 365, labor cost for the day, and what we purchase for the day in food, liquor, and supplies broken down. I always had to know if we made or lost money every day of the year. I purchased another 1 percent of the place and had controlling interest, so I had the right to ask. In other deals that I made, where I owned a smaller percent of the business, I made sure that in the bylaws of the corporation that the daily budget report was in there.

Most of my deals were smaller, but with the same goal in mind, to make money off someone else's efforts, someone else's credibility, and someone else's money. Whether it's a pizza place or a two-million-dollar carwash, the principle is the same. You're putting in money that doesn't belong to you in the first place and getting out money that you didn't do anything to earn.

Chapter 19

Making Money on Time-Share

ONCE WE PURCHASED A hotel in a seashore community for $40,000 per unit and converted it to condominiums and sold them for $150,000 a unit. We spent $10,000 a unit converting them to get though the township city fathers. We then turned the property into a hotel condominium. If someone purchases one, they were in the passive income bracket. Meaning that if you purchased one, it was like a business, the room rental vacancy factor was a write-off, the electric and gas bills were write-offs, the condo fees a write-off, and the average room was a $37,000 a year write-off. Everybody that ever bought a place down the shore bought one of these for the tax advantages. Plus, you could call up and say, "Don't rent my room this weekend, I want to use it," so you're getting a double use of it: rental income and personal use.

The rooms were very close to the casinos and rented for $80 to $100 a day. We were able to rent them out all the time so they eventually became also time-shares where one unit sold for $8,000 a week. The market was slowed now, but at the time, it was quite the thing. The hotel condo association charged 25 percent to rent the rooms and they were rented most of the time, especially in the summer and a banquet for weddings; many of the casino employers got married there because it was so expensive to get married in casinos.

There were several hotel condominiums built after that in the same area; our one hundred rooms sold out quickly, but the others that they built were hundreds of rooms and took a much longer time to sell or time-share. The idea on a small scale works well. There are many other places that you can convert to hotel condominiums; any apartment building or hotel condo building can be converted to hotel condominiums. Just think about how much money could be made if you purchased a hotel and converted it to time-share, and you paid $40,000 a unit and you sold the rooms out to condos in time share at $8,000 a week, times fifty-two weeks is $416,000 for a room and you only paid $40,000 a room. You would be selling out the building for more than ten times what you paid for; how's that for a real estate deal?

Hotel condos became popular in the early '80s, levelled off in the late '90s, and are presently a sporty construction ideal in this recessionary time that we are presently in. We should consider building them or buying an existing motel or failed condo development and converting it only in a recreational area, near a mountain or ocean resort. This might be the kind of place to try it today, some place with a high rental occupancy rate for at least five months of the year. Like I said, the tax write-offs are phenomenal for investors or users and the profit is very high.

Converting is relatively simple as long as you're willing to spend the money to convert the property into what you want to do. There are certain costs such as condo conversion cost and renovation cost in some cases. If you venture into this kind of project, you should study the costs beforehand.

Chapter 20

Finding Land and Making It Valuable

YOU ARE RIDING DOWN a state route, and you pass a large farm that's for sale. You notice that the land is on three different highways, and the property is about eighty plus acres. The price of the farm and land is about $350,000; that's less than $500 per acre. You count the footage of the front of the property and find it's about 2,500 feet long, enough for twenty-five lots across the front on three sides of the property.

You figure the lots are worth about $30,000 each. The fact that they are on the highway and not on the land tells you that they are improved, rather than just approved. Because you don't need roads to get into them, they are already on the highway. If the zoning is residential one acre lots, then you have twenty-five lots worth about $750,000. If the farmer is asking $350,000 for his farm, then you already made $400,000 without doing anything else, by selling the lots for $30,000 each. What you're going to do with the other fifty-five acres is up to you.

You could lease the balance back to the farmer to farm or you could build roads inside to get to the other lots and improve the rest of the property. Now you have already checked the zoning map to see what the land is zoned for or maybe you would like to get the zoning changed and get another use approved, whatever you do with the land is going to increase the rateable and increase the amount of taxes that you will give to the town, so you have a good argument to change the use of the land.

Maybe you would like to build an over-fifty-five community in the back of the lots that you sold off and built houses on, on the front of the property. The town would welcome you with open arms; the people who buy in an over-fifty-five units pay taxes, but they don't have any kids in school, so the township is way ahead of the game. Maybe your ideas are different; maybe you would like to build a shopping center, or an industrial park, or a trailer park—the opportunities are boundless.

Remember you purchase land with a purpose, not just to purchase it but to have a use for the land, to know what you're going to do with it before you purchase it. Then move forward with your plan.

You could also put some billboards on the front of the road to get additional income from the land, say one on the beginning of the land and one on the end of the land on the road that is the busiest. If you decide to build the houses yourself, you can make much more money. If you inform the seller of your plan, you can pay him with a performance mortgage, build a house, pay for a lot basis; if the seller has capital gains, then he can spend out the mortgage and pay installment tax payments to the government. If any of the land you purchased was landlocked (no access from the roads), it is possible to purchase an easement to get to it by contacting any land contiguous to the property.

Go into the township and look at the zoning map to get an idea as to what the property is zoned for; you might come up with a whole new idea. For example, if the property is zoned for commercial, you could build a commercial warehouse development. You build a 60,000 square foot building and subdivide it into 1,000 sq. ft. units; each one has a storefront with a warehouse in the back for distributing. A plumber that sells plumbing supplies to other plumbers or a company that sells computer ink or a company that sells wholesale refrigerators. Or a company that needs more space for storage of retired items that they want to get rid of. You would sell these subdivided units to sixty different parties for $100,000 per unit or $600,000 for the complex sold out. You would contact a plumber who works out of his home and sell him a unit that he can use to operate his business out of, with an office in the front and a warehouse in the back.

Chapter 21

Opening a Large Restaurant with Banquet Facilities

You find a large restaurant, hopefully a landmark restaurant, that's doing two or three million dollars a year. You manage to put down a payment on it and take it over; you can buy it yourself or do a syndication on it and contact doctors, lawyers, and businessmen that always had an idea to own a restaurant. They could take their friends to dinner at their restaurant, have their wife's birthday party at their own restaurant, or perhaps their daughter's wedding there. To do a syndication, you would put an ad in the paper, "Landmark restaurant syndication," and the professional people would call up and put maybe $50,000 or one hundred thousand in to the deal for part ownership. You would do a limited partnership with you as the general partner. You would be responsible for the operation, and you could do an agreement to buy the partners out after five years, after they've gotten their depreciation on furniture and fixtures, and use the money that you've made out of the restaurant for five years to purchase them out.

You would control the restaurant by doing weekly inventories and deposit every day in the bank exactly the amount of money you took in that day so that it's easy to account for everything. After five years, the restaurant will appreciate to probably double what you paid for it, making it a good real estate investment for you.

The reason you bought a landmark restaurant is so you can franchise it and maybe open a national chain, using this fifty-year-old restaurant's name. You would first do a management manual and then put the franchise in all the national franchise information centers all over the USA. When someone calls, go out to build the duplication of your restaurant in their location, charge them to build the restaurant, and then go home and collect your percentage of their gross.

Now as far as running the restaurant, you will use the fundamental restaurant operating systems such as the cleanliness system where each employee that come to work has a cleaning job to do on their shift. You will make up blocks on the weekly schedule, putting jobs in each block for each employee to clean a certain item or items in the restaurant that day. Maybe waitress 1 would clean the service station, the dishwasher cleans the Dumpster outside, the busboy cleans the chair legs, the cook cleans the prep area or whatever, that way the whole restaurant stays clean all the time. Learn to do a per person expenditure system, where each waitress keeps count of the amount of people she waits by adding up her checks at the end of the shift and dividing by her customer count and coming up with a per person expenditure (how much the average customer spent that day). If the waitress works twenty days a month, add up what the average customer spent and divide by twenty and see what her average customer spent to come up with the per person expenditure for the month for each girl. The girl with the highest per person expenditure for the month will get a $250 bonus.

When a customer comes in and orders a steak, the girl will say, "Would you like a side order of sautéed mushrooms for your steak, sir? How about a before-dinner drink? Appetizer? Dessert?" And so on. This will bring the girls per person expenditure up. Make sure that you inventory the liquor before the wedding and after the wedding so you can see how much you used and figure out your liquor cost per person.

This system will bring an average person's sales up to 20 percent; it's called interior marketing (once the customer is already in your restaurant, you're selling him more product). Linear scheduling system is a labor saver. By ringing the cash register when you come to work every hour and dividing by the people working that hour, you will get a man production hour system. If you took in $300 that hour and you have ten people working, then you have a $30-man production hour. So schedule everybody that comes in 24/7 to produce $30 per hour of business.

Learn this information so you become an expert at running your restaurant so you can write a management manual for your other restaurants. The idea of franchising has made many people billionaires over years, and it's the best real estate deal going. As far as the banquet goes, that's the best deal of all. Learn how to do banquets.

When you take over or open a new place, whatever the case may be, do a bridal show, winter, spring, and fall. Start out with a great fashion show showing off the newest grounds, bridesmaids' dresses, groom outfits, ring bearer dresses, and so on. Bring in at least twenty purveyors, the invitation guy, the travel agency guy, the limo guy, the real estate guy, the cake guy, the flower guy, the invitation guy, etc. Invite about three hundred brides. Everything free, champagne fountain, hors d'oeuvres.

Do a winter, spring, and fall show, you should get about ten or twelve weddings out of each show. Well worth it. When you book your weddings, if the wedding is $410,000, get $1,500 down and a $1,000 a month for a year, one hundred brides at $1,000 a month is $100,000 a month that you don't need for a year. For every $100,000,000 a year that you do, you're going to get a 20 percent gratuity that's $200,000 for every million you do. What a business, plus you're going to make a fortune on the weddings. At a wedding, you have 60 percent women and teenagers and 40 percent men. You're charging about $30 a head for liquor, and if you put carafes of wine on the tables, you'll keep them away from the bar. All this and you're going to franchise it. You can see what the potential is with this idea. Make sure you inventory the liquor before the wedding and afterward to get a per person cost.

Chapter 22

Building a Factory Is a Windfall

FIND A NEW BUSINESS to go into something that everybody needs and build a factory. In today's economy, you can come up with a product that everyone needs and wants. Find your location and purchase the land. Make sure you ran demographics and see what is needed in that area. Go to the EDA (Economic Development Authority) and out in for a loan, they'll probably give you 110 percent of what you need. Give them a list of the minority people you're going to employ: students, housewives, and other minorities. You need about 50 percent minorities to get the loan from EDA.

The EDA will probably finance a larger amount than you need, so don't be afraid of this deal. If the factory is in a zone, which is zoned as EDA target area, the state will give you the world, just because you're in that target area. Find some kind of product that people can't live without, such as furniture, lamps, appliances, car parts, something useful. You can purchase an existing building or build a new building. What is inexpensive is a steel building; perhaps a pastel steel or butler steel building would be appropriate.

These buildings are very sturdy and keep in heating and air conditioning very well. The equipment that you put in the factory will give you a five-year depreciation, which will help you with the amount of income tax you pay. The product that you make can be used all around the world, so don't forget to advertise it internationally. Buying a building or building a structure once you have a use for it makes the building and the business very valuable and will create a much higher value than you put into the deal. If you were to go public with the company, you could increase the value even more. You can sell the stocks off to individuals or form a bond issue, or if you're under twenty-five people, you could do a limited partnership, making yourself general partner, which means that you will control the company after you sold it off.

Finding a product that people need is as simple as running a graphic study to see how much of the product that you intend to manufacture is needed and how much of that product sold last year and the last five years. After you decide what product you want to manufacture, you will need distributors to sell your product to the public, who will make the product available online and in stores. If you're not able for some reason not to get all the money you need to build your factory, you can always borrow the money from a regular bank, as long as you use the bank for your depository (put your money in that bank every week).

There are many websites these days for selling products; it's not like it was thirty years ago. I have a friend of mine who manufactures lamps and sends them all over the world and the man is very famous for his lamps. By opening a factory, you are helping the economy and turning a buck at the same time.

Chapter 23

How to Put Together an Energy Company

Do YOUR RESEARCH ON windmills and purchasing energy-producing equipment? Do you research for purchasing the equipment to create energy to heat homes and supply electricity? General Electric, I think, would be one of the suppliers of windmills. Find a location for putting these pieces. Investigate the potential of building a power plant near a large residential area and plan to have the users participate in planning to use your energy to power their home.

I have this friend who lives in Florida who is growing trees in swamp areas to heat homes by using energy. The trees take two years to grow and the energy is consumed slower than the time it takes for the trees to grow. The operation is on only one hundred acres of land and will heat five or six thousand homes, generating a nice income for the developer. If you're able to heat a home and furnish power for less money, you will be an asset to the economy. The economic development in your state will do most of the financing for you, so it's not a lot out of pocket to create this deal.

There are many cities in the US that are paying too much for utilities; they would like to pay less. There are many different kinds of devices that produce energy; choose the one that works the best for you with wind power regulations, which have been built around fossil and nuclear resources and large hydro. These all need to be changed if we are to successfully promote climate solutions like comprehensive efficiency gains and solar, wind, geothermal, and bio wastes. A dozen or so individual states have taken faster action than the federal government, but it appears things are picking up steam.

This is most obvious in wind power. Now operational in more than seventy countries, wind power has been the fastest source of renewable energy. Worldwide wind power expanded more than fifteen fold over the course of the decade, from 4,800 megawatts (MW) in 1995 to installed wind capacity at 4,800 MW by the end of 2006. The wind market grew a record of 41 percent in 2005, and despite supply-clean constraints in 2006, it achieved an impressive $32 million growth. Some 150,000 people now employed in the global wind industry were responsible for the twenty-three billion in new generated equipment installed in 2006. Europe still leads the market, with nearly fifty thousand MV installed capacity: Germany (20,621 MW), Spain (11,603 MW), India (6,270 MV), Denmark (3,136NW), and the United States (11,603 MW), thirteen countries around the world, with France and Canada reaching the threshold in 2006. The cost of wind power has fallen drastically as the world market has expanded.

Today's wind turbine produces eighty times more electricity per year at less than half the cost per unit (KWH) than its counterpart of two decades ago. As a good location, wind can compete with the cost of coal or gas-fired power. I think I have given you an idea; now run with it. You're looking at the reason wind has become the fastest growing sector of the renewable energy market. GE Energy has done it again with wind turbines that are almost inconceivable in size and efficiency. Both onshore and offshore, they give utilities and electric cooperatives an attractive energy solution with minimal environmental impact.

Chapter 24

Going into Business for Your Self

I NEVER WORKED FOR anyone in my whole life, either I was under independent contract with large corporations or I was in business for myself. So I can tell you firsthand how to go about going into business for yourself, joining the self-employed is a big step for most people, to leave the security of a good job and take a shot at owning your own business. About seventy-five percent of all businesses fail in the first five years. Mostly because you don't have anybody to answer to but yourself, so how do you succeed where so many fail?

You want to be part of the twenty-five percent who make it, with sweat and tears, a lot of luck and hard work, unwavering courage, and mastery of detail. Important in a new venture, any size, is to investigate the business idea itself and your own abilities to run the new business. Look at the new product your selling or the service you are performing and see if it has a realistic chance to succeed in the marketplace. It's important that you have the knowledge and skills to handle the accounting, marketing, advertising, legal, and private matters. You must make a formal business plan for your own use and for the use of the bank or lending institution that you may deal with.

Most importantly, you must investigate the capability of the individuals who will manage, receive awards, and will share the loses with you. Be sure you have knowledge of the business and not just about the product itself. You must be able to trust the people who are doing your books and accounting. You've heard stories about bookkeepers taking the business over. Make sure you have hardworking, honest people around you. As far as legal papers required to start a business, find whether you want a sole partnership or an LLC.

Talk to a good attorney about what you want to do. Contact the city county and state to see what specific licenses are required to operate your type of business. It is necessary to have many legal documents executed also. You should have an accountant, a good lawyer, and maybe even a business advisor to ensure that your company is in compliance with city, state, and federal law.

In many cases, advertising ads suggest guaranteed success or that anyone can be successful in business. All businesses should be investigated and should be highly suspected. Most people who make money on deals are the ones that are selling them. If you do not understand how to start a business, contact the Better Business Bureau. The easiest to establish is a sole partnership. The owner is responsible for all the liabilities and places his personal assets on the line. A partnership is similar to a sole partnership, except that more than one person is involved in the profit sharing or management.

The other choices are the "C" or regular corporation and the "S" corporation. The difference between the two is in the taxation. In a "C" corporation, the entity is liable for the income taxes on gross profits before distributions go to the stockholders. The amount of the profit leftover after paying corporate income tax is then distributed to the stockholders as dividends and is again taxable to the individual as income. So the profits of the "C" corporations are taxed twice. In the "S" corporation, no corporate income taxes are paid, and the profits are distributed to the stockholders in the year earned. The individual stockholders then pay personal income taxes on those profits. The single reason for choosing a corporation is to protect the personal assets of the corporation's stockholders.

You should have a business plan to give the interested parties in a five-year projection of what your company will make in the next five years. A projected performer of how much you will make in the next five years and how you're going to do it. You can speak to a business broker to get a price as to what to sell your projects for. If I hired employees to work in my business, they would have an independent contractor's agreement drawn by me, spelling out their duties. This way you don't have to withhold any income taxes as every person pays their own taxes.

Chapter 25

Dealing with the Bankruptcy Court to Purchase Real Estate and Business

YOU CAN GO TO the bankruptcy court and look though their files and see if anybody is about to lose their real estate and or business or maybe both. There will be a large choice to choose from especially in this economy. The bankruptcy judge wants to dispose of the case as fast as he or she can no matter how big it is or how much business it's doing; they just want to dispose of it fast. It is very easy for a trustee to throw a case into chapter 7 after the people file chapter 11.

I had a friend who had a $2.7 million restaurant. He bought his partners out, but by time he bought it out, it was $100,000 in debt. The guy used all he had to buy the partners out. The state sales tax people and the IRS threatened to close the place up because the guy didn't pay his fire insurance policy for 1.5 months, and the trustee demanded that the judge make the debtor turn over his keys. The place was doing $50,000 a week in business, but with a $2.7 million appraisal, the guy lost the place and it was sold at sheriff sale for $1.2 million. It took my friend twenty years to build his credit back up. The same trustee went on to close down four huge food and beverage operations in about a year and a half, putting a couple hundred people out of work and costing the state many thousands of dollars in unemployment.

The state suffers from this trustee's greediness, but the government controls the bankruptcy courts. The bankruptcy court is brutal. If you watch cases, you can make the deal of a lifetime in the bankruptcy court. One man's loss is another man's gain. The first thing you can do is to advertise on the web that you purchase large bankrupt business and real estate; let them know that you purchase large companies and sell off the pieces, and people that are knowledgeable about certain cases will call you.

The best thing to do is to go in the bankruptcy court and go through the cases that are in the court. There is much information about the properties and businesses right in the bankruptcy file. You must go into court and try to make some sensible deal because if they don't give you the deal everybody loses. People have made large fortunes buying from the bankruptcy court. The bankruptcy court is a big hardship for most people, but it is a windfall for people who step in and get the great deals that are offered. The bankruptcy court is there to help people when they get in trouble, but more times than not, the people wind up losing everything they got.

There are basically two types of bankruptcy: chapter 13, which is personal, and chapter 11, which is for a corporation or business. Chapter 11 is supposed to be a reorganization plan, but with the wrong trustee, you don't have a chance to save your business. Once you file chapter 11, the trustee will do everything in his power to put you into chapter 7 and take over your business. The trustee receives a percentage of whatever he sells the business for, so he works with lawyers and professional people to get the place from the debtor and sell it at all costs. All the people that help him share in the high profits they make. This is an opportunity to buy a business for almost one-third to 25 percent of what the business is worth because of other people's greed.

You must first hire a good bankruptcy attorney to represent you in bankruptcy court. Line up your financing with the bank. Have a good manager with a resume lined up to manage the place if you don't know how to manage it yourself. You can always learn how to manage it once you acquire the business. If it's just a piece of real estate you're getting, then it's not important to prove to the bank that you can manage it. Once you acquire the business, you can run an impulsive marketing campaign to pump up the sales. If it's just a piece of real estate, for the bank's sake, you want to show how you're going to make it pay off. In this bad economy, it is the time to make your fortune, cashing in on other people's losses.

Chapter 26

Adverse Possession Is a Way to Foreclose on Properties

WHAT IS ADVERSE POSSESSION? Adverse possession is a long-term possession of real estate. Adverse possession is defined as not founded by a written instrument. An action for the recovery of real estate and a defense or counterclaim on title to real estate is barred by uninterrupted adverse possession of twenty years. A person, who, in connection with his or her predecessors in interest, has an uninterrupted adverse possession of real estate for twenty years, may commence an action to establish title under Ch. 841. Real estate is possessed adversely under this section.

Unfortunately for tax sale investors, the twenty-year prescriptive period makes this approach unattractive, especially for the investors wishing to "get rich quick" by buying and immediately selling the property. However, someone who is just interested in buying a house for pennies on a dollar might be willing to wait out the twenty-year period. This is a shorter period of time than the length of most mortgages today. This approach may be interesting to an investor who is looking for a home that can be turned into cash later in life. If the property is abandoned, then in effect he or she is giving the real estate.

Any offer for just pennies on a dollar might be viewed as found money. Look for houses that are deemed as a house that could be taken by adverse possession. Drive around, walk around, and look for properties that are neglected and unoccupied. When you find one, come back several times and see if there is ever anyone there. Days, nights, and weekends, is there anyone there? Are there lights on? Go up to the door someday, ring the bell. If anyone answers, you can tell him or her why you're there and see if they are interested in selling the property. Or you can say you have the wrong house, or pretend to be a traveling salesman going door to door.

If no one answers, go to the county records. Find out who pays taxes. If you really are interested in the property, then you can contact them and make an offer. If you find out no one is paying taxes, then find out how long they have been delinquent. Then go back to the property and talk to the neighbors. What do they have to say? How long has the property been vacant? Does anyone ever come around? If you get the answers you want that indicates that the property has indeed been abandoned, then you pay the back taxes and bring them current. Then take possession of the property, put up a sign saying that you own it, and that anyone else should keep out. Change the locks on the door, then advertise the property as a rental. If no one challenges you, then you have an income-producing property with no monthly payments.

You can borrow against it until you get the title. It is free and clear. You pay only property taxes and insurance, but that is not the best part. Most states have adverse possession laws, which allow people to take over abandoned properties and even claim title to them if the owner does not object within a specified period of time. Generally, the person who wants to take over the property has to prove that it was abandoned, and he took it over and used it flagrantly, openly, and in a manner hostile to the interest of the owner. To put it in simple English this means that you have to use the property openly and in a way that threatens the owner's ownership and control. Sneaking in there at night and sneaking out again every morning won't do it, not even living there openly. You have to challenge the owner's claim in some way.

Putting up a sign advertising yourself as owner will help establish your claim. You can put a fence around the property and do other things to discourage others from going into the property. If the owner cares, he must respond to your actions. He should send you a registered letter or better yet have his lawyer send it, warning you to stay away from his property or face legal action. About all you can get out of it is the money that you put up for property taxes and improvement. If the owner doesn't want to refund your money, you can always threaten to put a lien on the property. If you prove that you paid the taxes and improvements, you can put a cloud on the title. He will not be able to sell the property or borrow any money until the lien is cleared up.

Chapter 27

Purchase Business Cheap and Sell Them for a Profit

AFTER FORTY YEARS AS a business broker, I found myself many insolvent businesses that I would list for six months and purchase them myself or sell them to a beginner businessman. If I purchase it myself, it was probably for 25 percent of what is was worth. I would then put in a management team to do an impulsive advertising campaign and sell the business for four times what I paid for it. This in itself is a very good investment to get into.

I once bought a pizza place for $15,000 and sold it for $75,000 in one week. The guy that purchased for $75,000 gave me a deposit of $15,000, which I actually used to purchase the place with. I was able to clear $60,000 in cash in one week. I already had the buyer when I purchased the place. The seller was from one of the Middle Eastern countries and had a hard time making the place go. When you purchase a business, which includes real estate, it's good to move the business into a better location. With cheaper rent, if you can find a place. Then take the building and convert it into its highest and best use.

Another deal that I made was to purchase a deli down the shore. It was a summer operation. I took it over and put a manager in to run the place; we ran it for six months and made $40,000 on it.

You can look for good deals and even recently closed places, open them up, send out five thousand fliers. Have delivery, contact the local schools, give the school back $300 for every pizza that you sell, contact all the day-care centers in the area, add commercial catering to the menu. Do whatever you have to do to pump up the business; keep good records so you could show books. I purchased a day-care center; it was in a house next to city hall. I moved the day-care center which had fifty kids to another location. I made the place into a law firm because it was next to a hall and rented it out to a couple law students who had just graduated. I then formed an LLC and owned 51 percent of the law firm. What a lucrative project that turned out to be.

They went into court on Thursday night next door and handed out their cards, and now they have a busy law firm. There was a small custard stand down the shore and it was only open in the summer. But it was across the street from a large busy convenience store, so we opened it all year and put out better hoagies than the busy convenience stores across the street. We made a huge profit when we sold it several months later. Probably the easiest store to take over would be a dollar store, so find one that's insolvent.

You can purchase it cheap and even make a good deal on the inventory. Pump up the business where it shows a nice profit. Another way to purchase a business if you can get it cheap enough is to buy the business and sell off the place in parts; sometimes, that works even better. You can purchase newsstands, pretzel factories, bagel shops, company gas stations, and many other types of businesses and build them up and resell them for great profits.

Chapter 28

Foreclosing on Properties

THERE ARE MANY WAYS to foreclose on properties. The best and most profitable way is to buy ten tax sale certificates and foreclose on all of them. You're liable to get one or two. With the economy as bad as it is, there were millions of foreclosures last year in the United States. First, you would go to a tax sale and bid on the tax sale certificate. The actions are in every town in the United States one day a year. The tax sale certificates will pay you over 18 percent interest if you just want to sit on them. If you keep them for two years and the owner of the property doesn't redeem the tax sale certificate, then you can foreclose on their property. You have to pay all subsequent taxes on the property after you buy it, but you're going to get all the money you spent on the property when the owner redeems the property back if he redeems it or you will foreclose on his or her property. This is the cheapest way to get a property.

Another way to get a property is to go to a sheriff's sale; the only problem is there are a lot of other people bidding on the same property. The best way if you can do it is to go to the sheriff's sale and let somebody else bid on the property; find one who gets a great deal or a low price, then go to the owner of the house, give him a couple of thousand dollars to hand over the quitclaim deed to you, then go back and redeem the house back from the sheriff sale. Every state is different, but in a lot of states, it's two years before you can foreclose. After you buy the tax sale certificate after two years owning it, you may start foreclosure. Hire a lawyer and send out a notice to all that are involved in the foreclosure, giving them notice that you are starting foreclosure; this will tip off the people involved.

They will either redeem the tax sale certificate, and you will then make your 18 percent interest for your investment or they won't do anything and you start your foreclosure proceeding. After about six months and several more notices, the house will be foreclosed on. If there is a mortgage on the property, you will have to make a deal with the bank. If the mortgages for example are $60,000, then you're going to offer the bank say $25,000 to buy it out. Although if the bank did not object to your foreclosure, maybe they are just walking away from it, using it for a write-off. In any case, if the house is worth a couple hundred thousand dollars and you get it for $40,000, it's a deal. It is good sometimes to rent the property back to the former owners and let them pay the mortgage off.

You can also purchase the tax sale certificate, sometimes at a discounted price. If this is the case, you would register the sale certificate with the county that the property is in. After which, the tax sale certificate is in your name and under your control.

The owner has ten days to redeem his property back. Remember to do your homework and find out what the owner owes in taxes and mortgages, how many other people are involved in that property, maybe someone bought a tax sale certificate on the property last year and the owner never redeemed it. If you go to a sheriff's sale, that's an absolute sale there, everything is paid. You can read about tax sale certificates in another chapter of this book. Another way to foreclose on a property is to take over the mortgage; be the bank in the deal.

Find a property that has a mortgage on it, a second mortgage on it, and third mortgage on it. Buy out the first mortgage, then buy the second mortgage out at a discounted price because it's not worth as much because it's in second place. Buy out the third mortgage; it's worth even less than the second mortgage, so they should discount that mortgage even more. There are many ways to make money from purchasing tax sale certificates. You can just buy them for the 18 percent interest that they pay, which is guaranteed by the US government. You can become a tax sale certificate dealer by buying tax sale certificates and selling them for a profit.

To start a tax sale certificate dealership, you would need to meet with all the other purchasers of the certificates by going to tax sales, introducing yourself to the other dealers, and by making deals with them on purchasing some of their inventory. If you purchase ten certificates, you should be able to foreclose on one anyway. So you buy ten for $10,000 each, that's $100,000 you spent, already making 18 percent interest on them. Then you're going to foreclose on one, say $150,000 house, that you probably got $25,000 invested in, so you already made $100,000, plus you have the 18 percent on the other ones.

Chapter 29

Put a Syndication Together and Own the Property 100 Percent Yourself in Five Years

You first get on the phone and call all the high-income people that need tax write-offs. Get a list in your area of anybody that makes $350,000 a year. Find a large apartment complex that you can convert into condos or a large shopping center that is half empty that you can fill up and increase its value. Something you can buy cheap and turn it around. Once you have the place in contract, put an ad in the newspaper or advertise it online. "Syndication large complex, need five people with $200,000 each to invest."

You will want to do a limited partnership with you as a general partner. That way, you will control everything, make all the decisions, and make changes in the corporation without getting anyone else's permission. Make sure you structure the agreement so that you can buy everybody out after five years, after everybody gets the write-offs for the equipment and real estate appreciation for five years, which you will give your partners all the write-offs as part of the deal. After the five years, you can buy the other partners out with your share of the money you make in the venture, so in five years, you would own the whole project yourself.

Take the shopping center and make it more valuable by converting it into condominiums and selling the individual stores to your now tenants. You would sell the guy that's paying $4,000 a month rent for his fee simple store that he would own now, so when he goes out and gets a mortgage, it will only cost him $2,800 a month. Is he going to buy it? Sure, he is. Your deal when you take a shopping center and convert it to condos will make hopefully between $750,000 and a million dollars, which profit will be all yours in five years. You can accomplish the same kind of thing no matter what you choose to do, by taking any piece of real estate and converting it in to highest and best use, thereby increasing its value, making you the sole owner of this property after five years and winding up with all the marbles.

You can do any kind of deal you like, whether it's a building, a piece of land for development, or a hotel that you convert in to condos and sell out or time-share—the potential is limitless. Just be sure to spell out the terms and conditions of your deal, without leaving anything to the imagination so that nothing ever comes back and bites you on the tail. If it takes you a little longer to get the deal together, wait it out and make sure the personalities match your goals. Don't ever get in with people that are threatening, hostile, or want it all for themselves. Make sure you are dealing with professional people with certain goals and not hungry people that are only interested in walking away with the whole pie themselves. That's what you are trying to do; don't let anyone or anything alter your plans for success. It was your idea and they either live with that or you replace them right away. You don't need them, they need you.

When you're putting this idea together, you will need an architect and an engineer that will go into the township and attend meetings and get whatever approvals you will need to convert to condos or whatever you're doing, an attorney to draw all your paperwork and maybe for more representation in the township, and an accountant to do a performance for you with projected income for the project.

Remember, you hired these people, so they work for you, do not get anyone else in on the mechanics of your deal, you need total control of all the professional people that work for you and are putting your deal together.

Chapter 30

Putting Your Commission Back into Deals to Put up Your Part of the Money

THESE DEALS I AM telling you about in this book, I very seldom put any money myself. I would list a business for sale and then put my commission back into the deal. If I would sell a carwash for one million dollars and the commission was $100,000, I would put the commission back into the deal and the buyer who now is my partner would up $100,000 and run the company. My partner would get a salary for running the company and then we would split whatever was left. There is a lot of money in doing things the way I did, but you must be able to check on inventory purchases and track it. If you lose control of any business, it could break you.

If you're selling a motel to a group, for example, and they don't have the money to put down, you can put up your commission for down payment or part of it. You can join the venture and get part ownership or you can take a five-year payoff and collect monthly payments. If you're not a real estate broker, then you can be a business broker and you don't need a license in most states. The advantage of being a business broker is that when you go out to list a carwash and there is a building and a business. You, as a business broker, would just list the business and not the real estate because you're not a real estate broker.

If you're selling a large restaurant for an individual, you can always put your commission in if the buyer is short with the down payment; just to make the deal, otherwise, you don't sell the place you're not making anything. If you're having trouble selling the place, you can always syndicate it. That's easy, everyone wants their own restaurant. They can have their wife's birthday party there or their daughter's wedding at the place. They can say to their friends and customers or clients, "Come to my restaurant for dinner." To syndicate a restaurant, you would put an ad in the largest investment, one hundred thousand dollars, and buy a list of everybody that's makes $300,000 a year.

Send them direct mail, offer them the five-year depreciation on furniture and fixtures and the level depreciation on the real estate for a write-off. Do they want to give the money to the government or would they rather give the money to you, secured by real estate? If a guy makes $300,000 a year, he is paying about $84,000 a year in taxes. Get a list of everyone in your area and send out direct mail. Have a meeting once a week with your investors; make sure when you meet that they are all together, that they don't exchange telephone numbers and maybe do their own deal.

The seller will always list with a business broker rather than a real estate broker. The advantage is if you were the seller, would you rather list with a business broker and pay for the commission on the business only or list with a real estate broker and pay commission on the whole thing? If you are selling a large restaurant, the first thing you would do is call the restaurant chains and see if they are interested and then the individuals to see if they would be interested. You then do the demographics, check the area out, check to see if the place is at a corner where cars don't pass the place at fifty miles per hour since the best location would be at an intersection on a corner with plenty of traffic.

Gather area studies, then package it and send it to ten or fifteen national restaurant companies. Remember, in syndicating the place, you can always put the last $200,000 to make the deal fly. Of course, you can always take your commission and walk away from the deal or you can leave your commission in and take a five-year pay-out that's about $2,300 a month.

Chapter 31

How to Get Very Wealthy on Residential Real Estate Starting with Your Own Residence

STARTING WITH THE EQUITY in your home, you can gain so much wealth, but you must first go out and mortgage your house to the hilt. You then look for great real estate deals that are hard to find, such as people losing their home with a lot of equity in it. You approach these people losing their home and offer them a couple of thousand dollars to hand over the quitclaim deed to their house and leave the premises, sign the house over to you so to speak before they lose it. You may go to the sheriff sale, and someone buys a great house cheap; go to the homeowner and give him or her a couple thousand dollars for the quitclaim deed, then go back to the sheriff sale and redeem the house as new owner. The homeowner has ten days to redeem his house now that you are the new owner.

The next thing you will do is go and take out a mortgage on the new house you just bought and repeat the process all over again. Say for insurance, the house is worth $200,000 and you bought it for $80,000, you can borrow 80 percent loan to value on the house or $160,000. If you paid $80,000 for the house, then you get $80,000 in your pocket. Then you will rent the house out and the tenant will pay the mortgage. When you rent the house out, make sure you check the tenant's background. Run credit report, landlord history, how long he or she has been at their jobs, etc. Then go back and pay off the money you borrowed on your own house as soon as you can, you should be able to do the next deal for cash.

When you finance the next deal, you use the money to purchase another property and so on. Do not spend any of the money. This is your new business that you are making an investment in. In a normal market, the real estate will appreciate 12 percent a year, and if you buy $200,000 homes, they will go up $24,000 per year. If you have ten houses, then you will make $240,000 a year profit.

It will take you a couple of years to get in that financial situation, but what else are you going to do in that couple of years? Look at it this way, if you purchase a $200,000 home and you put down 10 percent, and it goes up 12 percent the first year, you made $4,000 that year, the next year you'll make $12,000 from the house. As long as you rent the house for enough money to cover the expenses, then you have a win-win situation. If you are buying an existing house from someone, you can make deals with discounts from the mortgages. The first mortgage you can get from 10 percent to 40 percent, discounted especially if the mortgage is from 40 percent to 70 percent if there is a second mortgage on the property.

You can have a plan on exactly want you're going to do with your house and in how much time. Remember, whenever you borrow money, you have to pay it back, and the law of diminishing returns will eat you up if you do not move quickly. If you get into a situation where you're not able to rent a house because of problem with the township about not being able to get a certificate of occupancy or many other reasons, remember you can always rent to section 8 (which I don't advise you to do) or you could sell the house. If you want to sell the house quickly, put it in multiple listings and offer the salesperson that sells it at $2,500 bonus at settlement. Every salesperson involved will bring all their clients to look at the house for that extra money to the selling agent. Remember, it's a matter of life or death to sell when you have to sell and buy when you have to buy.

Chapter 32

Buying a Marina and Converting It to Condominium Slips

BACK IN THE 1970s, I forget the year I was invited to a large condominium boat slip sale in a marina that was going bankrupt. This marina was built by the largest distributor of bulge pumps. The slips were going for three or four thousand dollars. I purchased five slips at the sale and sold them for $1,000 a foot whenever I sold them; first I rented them out for a few years before I finally sold them. The rent for the slips was between $4,000 and $5,000 a slip for a summer season and another $1,500 if they wanted to leave it in for the winter.

The marina rented them out for me and collected the rent for a small 10 percent fee. It's good to have the marina rent your slips out for you just to have them on your side if something doesn't work out for some reason. Like a big northeastern shore or something, a hurricane, any other catastrophic emergency, or someone bumping into one of your rental boat slips, when marina builders decide to go into bankruptcy. They bankrupt the corporation chapter 11 and they hold on to the condominium association and collect, after the bankruptcy, approximately two thousand dollars a year. Condominium fees just isn't a big deal for them since they get to collect the condo fees without paying a mortgage anymore.

So they are still way ahead of the game. If you ever get into that situation, you will know what to do. If you ever have to go into bankruptcy, get a good lawyer, otherwise the trustee will take everything you have. Well, that's where I got the idea to buy marinas and convert them into condominium boat slips. I went to the Chesapeake Bay to look at marinas for sale. It seems to be a popular place to keep your boat if you lived in Washington, DC, and Philadelphia. It seems to be a haven for boats forty-two foot plus, with many coves were you could anchor and look for prehistoric sharks' teeth and fish and swim and so on.

You could make a nice profit converting them and selling them out. The marinas whenever I went into it were selling for about $12,000 a slip. The cost to convert them was about $4,000 a slip to put in floating docks at the drop-down sea wall in front of the marina to stop the waves from coming in when the other boats pass. You can also build a marina and rent out the slips and just be a regular marina operation; it's still a good business. First, you build a marina, then you put in a clam bar and a bait-and-tackle shop. Then a ramp to put boats in the water and a boat stacker and buy a forklift to drop the boats in the water when someone calls. The boat stacker accommodates many more boats in the marina because you stack the boats up to five stories high.

Someone calls up and says, "I want my boat in the water at 3 p.m." You just have to grab the forklift, go to the boat stacker, take the boat down, and put it in the water. When the guy leaves, put the boat back on the shelf, so to speak. Along with the condo slips after you sell them out, you could have a boat repair business, sail boats service, and winterize boats, and put a couple boat franchises there. There's no limit as to what you could do with your operation.

Chapter 33

The Salesman

How good of a salesman are you? How far would you go to make a million dollars or five million dollars? In order to be a good salesman, first you must qualify your customers. Make sure that there is no doubt in your mind that the person you are trying to sell something to is qualified to buy it. As long as the person has the money or the means to buy what you want to sell, then I'll teach you how to sell it to him or her. You must investigate your potential investors; check them out to make sure they have the wherewithal to purchase the deal you're selling them.

It's a big waste of time to try to sell something to someone that would like to purchase what you are selling but he just can't; even if he is a nice guy that you would like to have for a customer, he just can qualify. Try to get a credit report on this person, a financial statement from his accountant, a track record of what he has done in the past, and his net worth. First, you must advertise whatever you're selling in the right place, large newspapers like the *Wall Street Journal* and the *Hong Kong News*. You want the wealthiest people so you can use the biggest and best newspapers.

Don't be afraid to talk to these people; you're selling the best deals in the world; sell your heart out. The more confident you feel, the better you'll sell to this person. The product you are selling is a highest and best use product, which you've already done the research on and it is exactly that. You just have to believe that before you sell it to someone else. Once you believe in what you're selling, it becomes easier to sell it. You must back up everything you're selling with research. Study the product and make it the best idea in the world.

Tell the investor about the profits that he can expect. Tell him about the tax write-offs he will receive. Make him see that he can't get hurt in the deal. Once you get a couple people in your deal, the driving urge will make you succeed. Make sure that before you meet with your potential investor, that you have all the figures from the accountant, the engineering reports, the architectural drawing, and all your legal planning in line.

Some people with money tend to treat you like you're a second-class citizen, disregard that person and go to the next one. Some people have more compassion than others and are much easier to talk to about your deal. Don't dwell on certain people who would give you a hard time. After all, it's your deal and it's yours to sell and keep. At this point, you have put a lot of time in your deal; don't spend time with the wrong people, only the positive ones that are for real. At this point, you've done renderings, concepts, performances, and a huge presentation schedule.

Chapter 34

Land under Valuable Property

I KNEW A GUY one time that bought a piece of land in the path of development before the developer decided to purchase it. The area that he purchased this land in was casino-zoned. The gambling was approved and came in two years after that; meanwhile, the guy sits on the real estate for two years. When they passed the referendum for gambling, the guy decided not to sell the land, and when the casino decided to build, he decide to charge them rent for the land, a 200×400-foot piece underneath the casino.

The guy paid $75,000 for the land two years before they approved gambling so that he would own it when the gambling came in to the area. The guy drew up a twenty-year lease for the two-hundred-foot piece that he owned under the casino for $75,000 a year, for the land which he paid $75,000 under the whole thing. The lease expired in 1991, so he renewed the lease for $250,000 a year after that for ten years. The lease expired in 2011, and then he raised the rent again, this time to $300,000 per year. Using a 10 percent capitalization rate, the property will be worth three million dollars, not bad for a $75,000 investment.

You can purchase land for a song before development comes in, but you have to be able to sit on it for a long time. Land with no income is very hard to hold on to. You must have a plan as to what you're going to do with the land. The best way to do this is to create a land bank, where people invest in the prospective future of land purchases for future return. In order to create a land bank, you have to come up with a good land approval for development plan. The guy that bought the casino property almost lost the land back to the bank because he had a bad year in 1973, when the economy was bad.

That year, 1973, McDonald's was up to 25 percent and the full service restaurants were down 25 percent. Many of the full service restaurant chains were closing up. Marriot Corporation decided to build up their gross volume in a bad economy. There was a terrific gas shortage that year; the cars were lined up at the gas pumps in droves. I remember I purchased a 240D diesel Mercedes and put an extra gas tank in it so I had a seven hundred mile range without stopping for fuel.

Back to the guy with the casino property after gambling came in on the referendum. I remember the guy purchased useless pieces of wetland properties on the way into where the gambling casinos where and put billboards up, about seventeen of them, which he still owns today. It was an 850-seat restaurant, which was also built in expectations of gambling coming in. The guy that had built the restaurant had a heart attack six months after it opened. The guy envisioned the casino being made out of existing restaurant. The area coming in was to be roulette tables and chap tables, and the other rooms were blackjack and slot machines. But as it turned out in those days, none like Las Vegas, nobody knew that you had to have five hundred rooms and 25,000 square foot of gambling area to open a casino. So my friend purchased the restaurant, and they knocked it down and built another casino on that site. Once again, my friend who refused to sell out to the casino got paid great money for his land underneath the casino. He bought the restaurant property on a lease purchase, just to get into the deal with not much of a down payment. Then he operated it for a while until they would decide to build a casino there.

When they decided to build a casino there, they formed syndication, but one of the guys in the group was an attorney who represented Al Capone in the old days, so the town refused to give the syndication a gaming license. The company that was building the casino said, "I'll never build another hotel in this state again for the rest of my life." Before they were turned down, they built a five-hundred-room casino, so the approved and built casino was sold to another guy who opened it. The new guy paid them $25 million more than it cost them to build it. My friend who owned the piece of land under the casino then leased it to the casino owner for $350,000 a year. The lease expired in 1994, and he renews it for another ten years for $450,000 per year, which expired in 2004, and which was renewed for another ten years for $550,000 a year. Using a 10 percent capitalizing rate, the land under the casino is worth $5.5 million, not bad for a $650,000 investment. So you see, it's not hard to become wealthy; you just have to be in the right place at the right time and decide to make the move.

Chapter 35

Time-Share a Large Boat for Obscene Profits

A FRIEND OF MINE from Florida called me and told me that he was buying a fifty-four-foot sailboat out of Hurricane Katrina and would I like to get involved in the ownership. I wasn't interested at the time, but he called me a year later and told me the boat was finished. My friend restored the boat like new and he was ready to charter it out, with him as a captain. He asks me if I wanted to sail over to the Bahamas with him and try out the boat and see what I thought. The boat was in Daytona Beach, Florida, so it was only a day's cruise to get to the Bahamas, so I decided to go.

We got underway, and it was the most beautiful experience I think I ever had. The cruise over there was like a dream. I don't know if you've been sailing, but standing in back of the steering wheel with the wind on your back, pushing this very large sailboat across the water in pristine fashion. You can feel the power of the wind behind you, it's just breath-taking. We moored off Grand Bahamas and took our dingy into shore. It was like you were in Monte Carlo or someplace going into a casino for the day, wonderful. We spent a week there and had a wonderful time. I decided afterward I like this life and maybe I want to be involved in this life a little.

I was older now and this is so relaxing. At night, we would stay on the boat, and in the morning, we would swim in the clear water, spear fish, or just bask in the sun all day with a cool drink. We started a charter business out of Daytona Beach. I went into partners with my friend. We had day trips to a lot of different places I had never been before and for one week at a time.

One day, I said to my partner, "Why don't we do a syndication to purchase some more boats and maybe time-share them or give fifty people a week each and let them own a boat like ours?" We purchased another large boat out of another hurricane, fixed it up, and did a time-share of it with fifty people. Each person would take the boat for a week, at a time. If they didn't know how to run the boat, we would charge them $1,000 a week to captain the boat for them.

We paid $55,000 for the wracked boat. It cost about $50,000 to fix the boat up, but when we got finished, it was worth at least $250,000. So we sold fifty weeks of time-share for $10,000 a week or $500,000. The time-shares were interesting to people who didn't want to spend $300,000 for a boat. With the time-share, we included slip fees and insurance, so you get a boat for as much time a year as you use it. Plus, the tax write-offs are great; we gave them to the purchasers of the time-share. If your income bracket was great, it wouldn't cost them too much money. That was five years ago; we've done the same thing several times and made a very successful business out of this idea. Just another idea for you, and remember you can always syndicate this deal if you don't have the money to do it yourself.

That's the whole idea of my book. Deals like this make a lot of money. You can time-share anything you like. For example, with the boats, you probably only use the boat for a few times in the warm months anyway, so it doesn't make sense to purchase a boat, buy insurance, and pay for slip fees. It is basically the same as real estate except it's a boat rather than a condo or whatever. To buy a boat like what we are selling in time-share would cost you $500,000 for the boat, $7,000 for the seasonal slip fee, winter storage, and winterizing, and proportion for putting back in the water every year. Wow, what a bill. This way you're just paying $10,000 for every week you use the boat, one-time payment. Slip fee, insurance, and everything else is all paid for.

Chapter 36

Warehouse to Mini Storage Conversion: Six Dollars a Foot Income to Twenty-Five Dollars a Foot Income.

You ride down a busy interstate, looking down at warehouses and factories. You see a big warehouse for sale, maybe 150,000 or 200,000 sq. ft. You copy down the number and make the call. You can purchase the warehouse for three hundred and fifty thousand dollars. You then go into agreements with the seller with the contingency to get warehouse zoned for its highest and best use, which happens to be a mini storage. You get the approvals from the township and then you have to build 10×10 and 10×20 storage bins, allowing for 20 percent of the space for hallways and turns. You go to a township meeting and try to get approval. It's better to hire an attorney and an engineer to go with you to get these approvals to convert this warehouse into a mini storage.

The reason you are on a freeway is because 200,000 cars a day go by and see your warehouse, which will have a big sign on it, Cheap Mini Storage. That you can give you the maximum exposure. You will then have your engineer and the architect that you now have to begin the layout for the floor plan. Then when you have the blueprints, you can contact a construction company to build your project out. You're building self-storage bins that can be made out of wood, metal, plastic, or whatever material you choose. You must have hallways to get into each individual unit, with room for carrying carts to bring merchandise in on.

You must allow 20 percent of the square footage of the warehouse for hallways. You can choose to have heated or non-heated spaces. Your exposure will be a large sign on top of the building that 250 thousand cars a day will see from the interstate. Cheap Self-Storage. Then you will charge eighteen dollars a sq. ft. a year rather than the normal $25 per sq. ft. a year like the normal amount for such service charges. You will then go out and purchase a couple diesel trucks to lend to you tenants free to load their stuff and bring it to you. Once they fill your bins with their stuff, then they're not going anywhere. Make sure you order a self-storage study on demographics and need for mini storage in your area. This is one of the highest end profit ventures you will ever get involved with. So move forward on this deal ASAP.

You will find that there are many deals to make money as you move though these pages. It cost much more to build a new storage complex although you could build one out of pastel steel or butler steel buildings, which are very inexpensive as compared to conventional buildings. There are several approved sites available; for information, contact the author of this book. The cost for buying a piece of land and getting approved could be a monumental experience; sometimes for whatever reason, someone will go through the approval process and not build after they get the approvals. You might be better purchasing an approved site rather than going through the process yourself.

Chapter 37

Converting a Warehouse into a Condominium Warehouse

You find a large warehouse for sale, hopefully surrounded by many small businesses. You want to look for the guy that's a plumber and works out of his home or the guy that owns an appliance store who needs more storage space. You will approach the warehouse owner and tell him that you would like to convert his warehouse into a condominium warehouse and sell them separately. In order to do this, you would need time to get approvals, so it will take you at least a year to go through the approval process and would he go into agreements with you for whatever length of time it takes to get the approvals from the township. After he agrees to do so, you will go into contract with him. You have to judge the seller and make sure he is not the kind of guy that once you give him the idea, he would do it himself.

If you think he would build it out himself, then don't tell him what your intentions are. Once you get into contract, you would go to the township with an engineer and go to township meeting and set forth your idea. Your meeting will consist of getting the township to approve your dividing the warehouse into a hundred square foot units to sell to individuals with individual business. You are going to give each man a thousand square feet, unless by doing the research and advertising your concept, you get a guy that wants more square footage, but not enough to ruin your concept. Assuming the building that you are using was one hundred feet wide, you would build two condo warehouses every twenty feet, back to back; the condos would be twenty feet by fifty feet or one thousand square feet. Each one would have a garage door and a pedestrian door. The garage door would open into the warehouse and the pedestrian door would open into the office.

It would be a commercial-industrial park with mixed zoning. The plumber, or electrician, or whatever the business is will operate out this complex rather than out of his house or wherever he was operating before. He can have a warehouse with all his goods and an office for customers to walk into. The best of both worlds to speak.

I would then market the idea to all interested parties, small business people mostly, but others who need space also. I would advertise upfront before I started building the project. I would make sure that I had at least fifty thousand square feet of interest letters to show the need to the bank that I had a slam dunk audience for my idea. When I got those interest letters, I would take them to the bank to get my financing in place and show them to any and all investors, partners, or anyone with a concern.

The first time I ever used this idea was back in the middle '70s. I was, at the time, director of food service at Dulles International Airport in Chantilly, Virginia. My soon-to-be father-in-law landed at Dulles to look at the warehouses that were built for Transpo 72, the big air show. My soon-to-be father-in-law had purchased the Supersonic Transport (SST) from Boeing in Seattle. To build an air museum in Orlando, Florida, he needed to build a T-shaped hangar to house the SST. He purchased the first jet engine from the inventor, a German officer by the name of O'Hiem, and he purchased the Spruce-Goose, a plane that was built by Howard Hughes, from the government. My father-in-law came to me one day and said he had one warehouse left and asked me to purchase it for the low price he was paying to the FAA for all the warehouses. I took the warehouse and subdivided it into fifty warehouse condominiums and sold them out individually.

Getting back to the warehouses, after you market them, sell them out individually. If you want to, you could purchase a used warehouse like I did and then you would have to disassemble it and rebuild it in your location. When I built mine, I subdivided them with cinder block walls, but today, it might be less expensive if you used a chapter material to build your separations.

Chapter 38

Converting an Office Building into Condo Offices

FIND AN OFFICE BUILDING that you want to convert into condominiums. Talk to the tenants and tell them instead of paying $4,000 a month for your office, you will now pay $2,900 a month and that they will own their fee simple piece of real estate. Once you get it in agreement contingent upon converting it into condominiums, you wait till the contract is accepted, then you go to the township and start to get your approvals to convert the building into condos.

If the building is empty, you must contact other people who would want to buy their own office real estate. You will go out and actually speak to other office renters about coming in and buying an office in your building. The advantage of buying your own office other than owning it yourself and getting all the tax advantages and the depreciation that goes with ownership is that if they ever move, they can sell the property at any time. They, as an investor, will make a great profit being the original purchaser of the unit store.

The advantage to you as an investor is that you'll make a great deal of money on the investment; a twenty-unit building should make you anywhere between $300,000 and a half a million. The profit comes when you sell out the building. If you hold on the condo association, you will wind up with a nice income afterward.

The best way to convert and sell out is to finance it yourself, that way you could get a down payment and hold a mortgage, and the advantage to this if you are able to do it is the capital gain taxes. As you receive the monthly payments, you can pay a minimum tax so that the capital gain taxes that you pay will be in installments rather than all at once. In order to make a building condo, you have to separate the units with cinder block, so in case of a fire, only the unit on fire will burn and not the whole building.

It will probably cost you about twenty or thirty thousand legal fees to do this, plus fees. A successful condo conversion is a very lucrative venture. The condo as so will bring you fees in years to come. If for some reason you don't have all the money to put this deal together, you can always syndicate it. Put an ad in the local paper that has a big circulation area. "Syndication large office condominium project, investors needed. Minimum investments $100,000." If you don't get anybody, drop the minimum investment price to $50,000, you'll just need more people.

Don't have more than twenty-six people; if you do, you'll have to do a bond issue and you'll be under the jurisdiction of the SEC (Security and Exchange Commission) or purchase an existing defunct company that's still on the shock market. When the people call up, set up a meeting with them to talk about the deal. Have blueprints, approvals, and a business plan for selling out the units. You would then form a limited partnership with you as a general partner. The limited partnership is one where you, the general partner alone, are responsible for all the liabilities of the corporation, the only thing the investors would lose is the amount of money they put in to the group.

Chapter 39

Making an Apartment Building into Condos or Co-Ops

FIND YOURSELF AN APARTMENT building that you want to convert into condos or co-ops and put it into agreements of sale. Tell the seller that you want to convert the property to condos or co-ops. And that you will have to tie up the property for about a year to get your approval process done. And would he mind waiting for your approvals? If he agrees, have the agreement signed before you start. Remember you don't have to purchase real estate to control it, you just have to have it in agreements of sale to control it. As long as you do everything on that agreement, the seller can't get out of the deal. That means, while you have it in agreements, if you want to syndicate it, flip it, or whatever, you are able to.

Make sure when you do the agreement, you word it properly, such as Robert Domico, assignee or nominee of New Jersey Corporation to be formed here after known as a "Buyer." That way, if you decide to do something different with the property within that year when you're getting your approvals, you can. If you can figure out any way to tie up a property for a year, you can do whatever you wish with the property. There is enough profit in converting the property that you're not going to argue over the price. You want the seller to think he is smarter than you when you sign up the deal. Again, if you would like to syndicate this idea, you can put an ad in a large newspaper. "Syndication $100,000 minimum investment."

Now you're going to start your conversion into condos or co-ops. Go to the township meeting. Bring your lawyer with you and tell the township want you intend to do with the apartments: convert them into condos.

You have to build a concrete wall between the units to make condos, so if one unit catches on fire, just that unit will burn and not the neighboring units. On the other hand, if you make it co-ops, you may be able to get around that extra construction. The difference between condo and co-ops is with the latter instead of separating the units you just form a corporation. If there are one hundred units, then each owner of the units owns 1 percent of the corporation. Now you are going to the meetings to ask if the apartments can be converted into condos, the advantage for the town rateables (taxes) will be increases with fee simple ownership as opposed to the present situation with the present tax structure.

Once you get your approvals, you begin construction of separating the units into condos. You will bring in your engineer to design the units, whereby separating them as part of the approval process. Your architect, if you desire, will change the interior design of the units to be marketed at the highest price. The condo idea is the highest and best use and brings in the most dollars that the condo conversion will bring. When you start to market your condos, advertise them in the local newspaper first, and if you don't get enough response, broaden your advertisement to a larger area. Remember, if you don't sell enough condos, your conversion effort fails and you will have to go back into the rental business again.

Chapter 40

Resort Area Condo Conversion and Hotel Condos

Perhaps the best type of condo conversion you can possibly do is to convert a hotel into condos, making them hotel condos. There you have the best of both worlds, you have a full service hotel and you have hotel condos at the same time. What you're going to do is get zoning changed from hotel to hotel condos with the township. This allows you to sell the condos out and still have a hotel business there.

In 1976, a friend of mine purchased a one-hundred-unit hotel on the beach and converted the rooms into condos. He paid $30,000 a room when he purchased the place and sold them out for $110,000 a unit. And still, he rented out rooms for the owners and charged the owners 25 percent of the room's rental for renting out the rooms.

So you purchase a hotel and sell all the units out and you still have a hotel business. The advantage in a person buying one of these units is that if you're going down to the shore that weekend, you call up and reserve your room; otherwise, if you're not going down this weekend, you rent it out and now you have a rental property, which is in the passive income bracket, like you have a business. As an investor, you can write off the vacancy, the electric bill, the gas bill, the property taxes, and the amount you pay the owner of the hotel for renting the room.

Your write-off could be as high as $37,000 a unit a year. That makes you want to buy more than one unit. Now if the hotel operation will allow you to time-share, then the income will go off the charts. Imagine paying $110,000 for a room in a hotel and time-sharing it for $10,000 a week or $500,000 year. How would that be for an investment? In this book, there are a few ideas on time-shares; read on. The hotel condo is a special deal where you can pay about $40,000 a unit and sell them for probably $110,000 or $125,000 depending on the area and the need.

Again, you must tie up the property for a year to get approvals. The cost could be between $30,000 and $40,000 to convert depending on the structural improvements required and the amount of aggravation the township gives you. Basically, you are converting rooms into fee-simple residences. If you want to syndicate your idea, it's the easiest to do because of the amount of profit it makes. And the write-offs for the people who purchase them.

Chapter 41

Building an Over-Fifty-Five Community

You look for a piece of land, preferably out of town on a highway with easy access from the city, at least maybe five acres or so, with shopping close by and maybe a mall within ten miles. You go into agreements to build an over-fifty-five community and contingent of being able to get the approvals from the township. You must get approvals for the deal to go though so you're going to tie up the property for at least a year. After you find your lot and go into agreements, you go into the township to a meeting with your lawyer and start the approval process.

The township, once you tell them what you're going to do, they will welcome you with open arms. You're building homes for people over fifty-five, so they pay taxes but they don't have any kids in school; what a deal for the town. You get your approvals and you hire an engineer to do your site work and lay out the areas that you want to build on. You plan to build more than one hundred units. Then you hire an architect and draw your renderings and start to design your complex. You set an approximate price and start to advertise as soon as possible so you can get a dozen or so commitments. Now you're ready to get the ball rolling.

You advertise in all the over fifty-five magazines and newspapers, in all the over fifty-five organizations, and of course in the local newspaper. You try to get the financing lined up for the purchases of the individual units. Line up the end loans for the buyers so that they won't have to go crazy lining up their own financing. You want to make it interesting for them so you might decide to put a small but adequate recreation center in. So your new buyers would have a place to invite their families in for to gatherings and reunions and so on.

If you can find a scenic location near a lake or a river, that would be even nicer than an open field location. If you don't have all the money you need to build the project yourself, you can form syndication. Put your ad in a large newspaper and write, "Syndication minimum investments $100,000 over fifty-five community project." Line up your meetings and present your proposal to the group and put it together. You're better off on your own and to do your thing, but you do whatever you can. Your success will start the day you put the deal in agreements, so start today.

Chapter 42

Develop Empty Land

You're riding down the road in a rural area and you see a large farm for sale. The farm has three road frontages and the farm is over one hundred acres; you decide you want to buy it. You measure the three road frontages and decide that's its perfect for making a fast buck on. The frontage measures about eight hundred feet, which you figure you can put fifteen building lots on the road. And because it's on a road, it is an approved building site because you don't have to put any roads in to get to it; it's already on the road. You begin to price out the lots; sixteen one-acre lots at $40,000 each is already $640,000.

The guy is only asking $350,000 for the one hundred acres; already you made $290,000 on this deal. You can buy the property, subdivide it, and lease the farm back to the farmer, or you could take your $290,000 profit and put roads into the land and build more lots, then develop the whole piece. If the land is zoned for one-acre lots, then you have to get the other lots that are not on the road improved by putting roads into them. Figure out the cost of putting roads in and try to get them. Figure you're going to lose about 25 percent for roads, so you can get a total of seventy-five lots on the one-hundred-acre site, seventy-five lots at $40,000 each is three million dollars. If the roads cost $150,000 to put in, you already made over $2.5 million. Now if you want to develop it, that's a whole other ball game. Pull in your contractor and start to build a couple simple homes on the front lots. You're on a highway with thirty thousand cars a day going by, so they will stop and look at your simple house and the houses will sell themselves.

If you decided after much thought to build a shopping center on the road and maybe a professional building and then some townhouses, some detached and some semidetached homes, you would change the whole configuration of the property. You might even want to make the whole thing an individual park if you could change the zoning. You would have to get changes made with the township. Remember, they need rateables (taxes) to grow their community.

Whatever you do with this site, you're going to make money, so move forward and build something. Take time and go to the township and ask them what they think they need in the area; sometimes they can come up with a better idea than you have, not being from the area. Once they come up with the idea, do you think they will approve it for you? You can make a good deal if you're in a rural area if you look around for them; research the area, talk to some people, go to the township, and check the zoning map. Find out what type of construction is needed in the area, check and see the demographics, find out where the businesses will come from.

Chapter 43

How to Do a 1031 Exchange

What is a 1031 Exchange?

It's known as IRC Section 1031.

A real property owner can sell certain property and then reallocate the proceeds in ownership of a like-kind of property and defer the capital gain taxes. To qualify as a like-kind exchange, property exchanges must be done in accordance with the rules set forth in the tax code and in the treasury regulations. The 1031 exchange can offer significant tax advantages to real estate buyers.

Who should consider a 1031 exchange? If you have real property that will net you a gain upon sale (generally), property that's has been substantially depreciated for tax purposes and/or has appreciated in fair market value, then you are exactly the person who should consider a 1031 exchange

There are five tax classes of property:

1. Property used in taxpayer's trade or business
2. Property held primarily for sale to customers
3. Property that is used as your principle residence
4. Property held for investment
5. Property used as a vacation home

Section 1031 applies to the first and fourth categories and sometimes the fifth category. Business use is defined as "to hold property for productive use in trade or business." Property retired from previous purpose of productive use in business can be qualifying property. Investments purpose is defined as real estate, even if unproductive, held by a dealer for future use; or the increment in value is held for investment and not primarily for sale.

Investments are passive holding of property for more than a temporary period, with the expectation that it will appreciate. Property held for sale in the immediate future is not held for investment.

Why should you consider a 1031 exchange? Defer paying capital gain taxes. A property structured exchange can provide real estate buyers with the opportunity defer all or most of their capital gain taxes.

Leverage
Upgrade or consolidate property
Diversify
Own multiple properties rather than just one.
Relocation into a new area.
Difference in regional group or income potential.
Change property types among commercial, retail, etc.

What are general 1031 exchange rules?

The real property you sell and the real property you buy must both be held for productive use in a trade, or business, or investments purposes and must be like-kind. The proceeds from the sale must go through the hands of a qualified intermediary and not through your hands or the hands of one of your agents, or else all the proceeds will become taxable.

All the cash proceeds will be reallocated to the replacement property. Any cash proceeds that you retain will be taxable. The replacement property must be subject to an equal level or greater level of debt than the relinquished property, or the buyer will either have to pay taxes on the amount of the decrease or have to put in additional cash funds to offset the lower of debt in the replacement property.

Disclaimer: There are substantial risks associated with the federal income tax consequences of purchasing and owning real estate property, especially if the purchase is part of a tax-deferred exchange under section 1031 of the code. In addition, the income tax consequences may differ depending on individual tax circumstances so each prospective purchaser must consult with and rely on his own independent tax advisor concerning the tax consequences of such a purchase and his individual situation.

The 1031 Exchange is an exchange of property in which capital gains tax deferral is available to real estate owners who sell their investment, rental, or business real estate and reinvest the proceeds in qualified replacement properties. The replacement property must be similar in nature—to be used for investment, rental, or business and therefore considered a "like-kind."

Property owners may sell and replace like-kind properties and defer taxes on the profits by meeting the requirements of Internal Revenue Code (IRC) for 1031 exchange properties. Sellers of 1031 exchange properties have a maximum of 180 calendar days from the time of closing of the initial sale of the relinquished property to complete the exchange into their replacement properties. Within the first forty-five days after the close, a seller must designate replacement property and properly identify them in compliance with IRS regulations. This most frequently is done by using a qualified intermediary, also known as an exchange accommodator.

There are three rules identifying replacement properties for 1031 tax exchange, the most common is the three-property rule, which states that the seller may identify up to three replacement properties regardless of their value. The second rule is that the seller may identify any number of replacement properties, but the combined value may not exceed two hundred percent of the value of the initial property sale. The third rule for identifying replacement properties is a number of properties of any value may be identified as long as the final value of the properties exchanged is equal to ninety-five percent of all the replacement properties identified.

The funds in a trust account with qualified intermediary can be used as deposit or earnest money in the purchase of the designated replacement property once all IRS requirements for the 1031 are met. If no new properties are identified in the first forty-five days and no designated transaction is completed during the full 180-day period, the funds in the trust account will be liquidated and the sale proceeds taxed at the prevailing state and federal capital gains and depreciation recapture taxes.

Many investors don't take advantage of the 1031 exchange because of the fear of the forty-five-day identification period. This fear is supported by numerous horror stories of failed exchanges and the devastating taxes that result from such failures. With proper planning and the right resources, investors can navigate the waters of the 1031 exchange and frequently double or triple their investment income while diversifying their portfolio, thus reducing risk. The key requirements are a good grasp of exchange process, a clear set of investment objectives, and a plentiful and consistent source of quality replacement properties.

Chapter 44

Beware of Real Estate Fraud: IRS Is Watching

FEDERAL INVESTIGATIONS HAVE IDENTIFIED an increase in frauds and schemes in the real estate business. These schemes victimize individuals and businesses, including low-income families lured into loans they cannot afford, legitimate lenders saddled with over-inflated mortgages, and honest real estate investigators fleeced out of their investment dollars. Special agents with IRS Criminal Investigation are uniquely equipped to investigate these types of mortgage fraud and illegal real estate crimes because they are skilled financial investigators whose mission is to "follow the money."

Some of the common real estate fraud schemes include: 1) property flipping—a buyer pays a low price for property and then resells it quickly for a much higher price. While this may be legal, providing false statements to the lender is not; 2) two sets of settlement statements—one settlement statement is prepared and provided to the seller, accurately reflecting the true selling price of the property. The second fraudulent statement is given to the lender, showing a highly inflated purported selling price. The lender provides a loan in excess of the property value, and after the loans are settled, the proceeds are divided among the conspirators; and 3) fraudulent qualifications—real estate agents assist buyers who would not otherwise qualify by fabricating their employment history or credit record.

The income earned from these types of real estate fraud schemes is often laundered to hide the money from the government. Money laundering is simply a process of trying to make illegally earned income appear to be legitimately earned. IRS Criminal Investigation follows the money and collects evidence; IRS agents forward their investigation to the Department of Justice for criminal prosecution. If criminal investigation is not warranted, the IRS can also take civil action. Each year, the IRS audits thousands of tax returns involving individuals and entities associated with real estate business.

The IRS hit list of real estate. If you want to transfer real estate within your family, does the IRS need to know? Regardless of the value of the property or if the money is being exchanged, the answer is "most likely." The IRS has been checking real estate transfer records in at least fifteen states. So far, the new initiative has netted more than five hundred cases for audit, and there will likely be many more depending on the results of the taxes collected from the initial effort. Similar initiatives are likely, as the IRS is budgeted to receive additional funds to seek out other tax cases of unreported gifts and income.

All US citizens or residents must file Form 709, United States Gift Tax Return, whether or not any gift tax is due, in the following situations: 1. If you gave monetary or property gifts totaling $13,000 or more to anyone other than your spouse in 2011, unless specifically exempted; 2. If you give gifts of farther interests in property, even if less than $13,000; and 3. If you are splitting the value of a gift with your spouse, even if your share is less than $13,000.

The IRS estimates that between 60 to 90 percent of taxpayers who transfer to real estate for little or no consideration to non-spousal family members fail to file IRS Form 709. Consideration is the money or property one would pay to another for the purchase of an asset. For example, if you transfer ownership of your house to your child and their spouse for $500,000 when the house is really valued at $1,000,000, you have gifted the difference in value of $500,000. This transaction is considered a gift because the property was transferred for inadequate consideration (would you have sold the home to an unrelated party for $500,000?). In this scenario, you should file a Form 709, listing a net of $500,000. Assuming you are unmarried, have no lifetime exemption remaining, and have made no other gifts to your child and their spouse, you will pay a gift tax on $474,000 ($500,000 less the $13,000 annual exclusion to your child and the same amount to your spouse).

What are the consequences of not filing a Form 709? The penalties can be quite severe. Consider not only the gift tax to be collected by IRS but penalties and interest as well. The IRS can assess an additional 5 percent of the gift tax liability for each month the gift tax return is late, up to the total maximum penalty of 25 percent of the tax due on the return. This late filing penalty is in addition to the penalty for paying late, which itself is in addition to statutory interest. Criminal prosecution is also an option of the IRS. The statute of limitation on gift tax collection does not start to run if no gift tax return was filed.

Using the example of your $1,000,000 home, if you timely file a gift tax return reporting the market value at $500,000, the IRS will only have three years to question the value of the gift. If you do not file Form 709 reporting this gift, and ten years later, the IRS determines that the fair market value of the home was actually $1,250,000, then you will owe additional gift tax, penalties, and interest. As you can see from the example, getting the statute of limitations clock running is in your best interest. Also filing the Form 709 does not necessarily increase the likelihood that your income tax return will be audited. Roughly $250,000 gift tax is filed each year. However, your statistical chances of having a gift tax return audited are less than 1 percent.

The IRS is motivated to collect taxes, interest, and penalties whenever it can. Given the status of the US economy and the resent bolstering of IRS budgets and personal, the IRS is being charged with bringing in more revenue for the federal government and auditing gifts of real property is one example of a more aggressive IRS. While you may consider your transfer of property a family affair, the IRS sees things differently. When in doubt, consult your tax professional.

Chapter 45

Import-Export Business

WHEN EXPORTING AND IMPORTING, you should concentrate on items that are very rare in the USA. My friend decided to build a small plant to make handbags out of the various skins that the locals could catch and bring to the plant.

To start, first you must buy an airplane to transport items from foreign counties. You can bring items like crocodile skin and mahogany. You will then build a small plant to make products out of the various woods that they have and the actual wood itself for boat building and other uses. You then make a deal with the heads of the interior who will pay their people to bring the items to make the products that are interesting to the US. You will open your own handbag company in the US and have store outlets in all the malls. You can sell your high-end items with your own labels and get into all the big stores with your items that not too many people have. And create a market of your own.

On the return trips to other countries, you can also bring items from the US that they don't have over there. Kind of make some US trade like it used to be in the old days. There are many items manufactured in the US that are much needed in the underdeveloped countries you'll be flying in and out of. A lot of items like fruits and vegetables are grown in foreign places, which you could also import while you're flying your planes back and forth. You should plan to live in these countries for a while to establish this balance of export and import.

Chapter 46

Mortgage Cash Flow Notes

A GOOD BUSINESS IN bad times.

If you sell a house, not being able to sell it any other way, and the buyer for whatever reason cannot get a mortgage on your house and you are forced to hold a mortgage, this is called a purchase money mortgage. The buyer is a good payer of monthly mortgage payments; he has a good job but cannot get a mortgage. Getting a mortgage today is very difficult. You need a good credit score. Otherwise, your interest rate will be too high. The person that sold the house wanted to get cash out, maybe to purchase another house or to go into business. For whatever reason, he wants his or her money out. In this situation, the seller, who is now the mortgage holder, is willing to discount the mortgage to get their money out.

Your new company will list the mortgage for sale, advertise it, and sell it to another party for more money than the person who is selling it is asking, making your profit. Example, the seller sold their house for $100,000. He took $20,000 down and financed $80,000. Now he wants to cash out of his mortgage and is willing to take $65,000 cash for the mortgage. You advertise the mortgage for sale for $75,000, and when you sell it, you make $10,000 profit. If you do four a week, you will make two million dollars a year. Other types of funds such as someone gets an endowment, a structured settlement, or hits the lottery for a pay-out and wants to cash it out at a discounted price.

These types of things are called cash flow notes. When someone wants to get their money out fast and is willing to discount it, that's where you make your money. As you go along, the tighter the economy gets, the more business you will do. You can create a website to advertise your cash flow mortgage notes for sale, and buyers and sellers of these mortgage notes will call you. Your business will take off like nobody's business. You just have to take the first step to make it happen. And guess what, you don't need any money to start this business. All you need is a cell phone and a room with a desk and a computer in it.

The best way to get started is to find a property with three mortgages on it. The first mortgage you can't do too much with, but the second mortgage can be discounted because it's less valuable than the first mortgage, usually about half. The third mortgage is even less valuable than the second mortgage, so you can discount that about a third. Every time you discount a mortgage, you're making more money on the deal.

The buyers for the notes can be banks, mortgage companies, and private investors, anybody with money to buy the notes. If you want to, you could put together syndication to raise the money to get started and you would get a percentage to manage the deal for the group. Wow, what a deal. You can easily make a million a year out of this deal with no money. Don't wait another day; start this company right away. The discounted mortgage market makes a lot of money because most of the time the good deals are from people who have no control over the mortgage, like if they are in bad times and are losing the house, or somebody passed away and there is an estate that nobody can control, or husband and wife break up, or partners in real estate disagree, or whatever emotional situation occurs.

Chapter 47

Starting a Home Loan Modification Company

IN TODAY'S MARKET, WITH all the foreclosures in the US, you could easily start a home modification company. The government has asked the banks to help with people's loans to wave the payments behind and re-cast the loans at a lower interest to help the situation along. Many banks are going along with the request. The banks are asked to reduce at least 10 percent and bring their interest rates down to 5 percent to save the economy. Many banks have agreed to help.

You would need about two hundred square feet of office space, with about ten desks, ten computers, and a commercial on line hook-up like Comcast class. You will need an office manager with some experience operating and repairing computers and general knowledge of computers to teach the salespeople how to operate the computers and help them do their job.

So now you come along and start a home modification company and help these people save their house. Do you think you would get any takers? I think so. After you set up your office, you would need an attorney to contact the bank and make a deal with your client's mortgage payments. You would pay the attorney about $500 per mortgage. You would then pay the mortgage modification salesperson an amount to service the account that they are working on. You would create a website to help people who are losing their home, save their home through home modification.

You are paying the lawyer and the salespeople on a sticky commission basis so you have nothing to lose. If you wish, you can hire a company to give you leads to contact people who are behind on their mortgages. After you set up your office, you can train a processor to handle the banks and set the deals with the banks to process your home modification; the commission you will pay your employees will probably be about 20 percent of your total fee that you charged the homeowner. The amount of the fee is usually one month's mortgage payment.

Many people are taking advantage of this type of business these days when foreclosures are high. Be careful to only charge an application fee upfront because if things move a little slow, people will start complaining to the attorney general's office and this can cause a problem. Remember, people are quick to complain when things don't go their way. Even though you are doing them a big favor, they won't see it that way. After all, they're broke and behind in their mortgage. And they are a little desperate. How long will it take you to save their house? You can't answer; just remember, they need you more than you need them. You are in a business that can potentially make a lot of money for you, so be patient.

Chapter 48

Heir Hunting, Deed Raiding, and Redemption without Cause

When trying any of these actions, be sure you don't have any licenses to lose.

If you're a real estate broker, a lawyer, or an accountant, you might want to watch your back on these deals as they might be construed as illegal in some states. There is always some lawyer out there that says you are committing fraud or you're taking advantage of someone, so make sure everything your doing is legal in your state. In one state down south, a couple of lawyers sued a tax sale certificate dealer, who was buying and selling tax sale certificates for a profit. The lawyers said they were making too much money selling them. I don't know how, but the lawyers won the case.

The dealers said you can make $5,000 on a car, $10,000 on a boat, and $20,000 on an airplane, but you can't make $3,000 on a tax sale certificate. The lawyers won the case, the tax sale certificate dealers decided not to go to the tax sales anymore, and the state wound up with a billion dollars-worth of tax sale certificates that they couldn't sell. Not to risk the state going broke, they guaranteed the buyer of the tax sale certificates 18 percent interest to purchase them. It was an expensive lesson to learn for that state.

So you see, there is always someone watching whenever you do something that's borderline legal. Find a lawyer that will guarantee you that what you're doing is legal.

In heir hunting, you call a person who is in foreclosure and ask them to sign the quitclaim deed over to you, maybe give them a couple thousand dollars. At that point, you own the house for better or for worst. You may want to run a search on the property to check out what's owed on it because you are going to have to pay everything off, unless you can make deals along the way. You might want to check in your state to see what's legal and what's not. Remember, it doesn't make any difference how large the property is and whether it's commercial, professional, or industrial. It's all real estate. The bigger the property is, the more you'll make on it. You could always change a warehouse into self-storage, a hotel into a hotel condominium, or a shopping center into condominium stores.

Deed raiding is going to a sheriff's sale, and when somebody bids on the property and they get a good deal on it, you go to the owner of the house and give them a couple thousand dollars and have them sign the quitclaim deed over to you. They have ten days to redeem the property back after the sale, so you as the new owner would go back and redeem the property. Again, make sure you run a title search on the property and get title insurance on it before you do anything.

Redemption without cause is done by an investor who will go on a tax sale and buy the tax lien. After the complaint has been filed and the tax lien is being foreclosed on, someone who is not involved will go out and attempt to acquire an old mortgage on the property or a deed to the property, then attempt to either compel the foreclosing lien holder to assign its interest; normally, the interloper will take away from the foreclosing lien holder most of the profit in the foreclosure.

Chapter 49

Getting Rich on Tax Sale Certificates

EVERY TOWN IN THE United States holds a tax sale certificate sale for one day a year as a result of one not paying property tax, water, or sewage bill. A tax sale certificate is created to be sold at auction to the highest bidder. Usually, the tax sale certificates start at 18 percent interest and are bid down, 18 percent, 17 percent, and so on until the lowest percent is bid. At that point, the high bidder will get the tax sale certificate for whatever it was priced or the amount of whatever the unpaid taxes were. You then have to pay all the future taxes, water, and sewerage, as they become due.

You will get in New Jersey 18 percent interest on whatever you pay. Whatever the percentage was that you bid is how much interest you will get when the certificate is redeemed from the owner of the property. Every state is different. But for example, in New Jersey, if the owner of the property does not redeem the tax sale certificate in two years, then the owner of the certificate can begin foreclosure on the property. The owner of the certificate in about six months after he starts foreclosure will own the property, unless the property owner redeems the certificates back and pays all lawyers' fees spent by the foreclosing certificate owner.

With the amount of foreclosures in the last couple of years in the US, you have a good chance of the homeowner not redeeming his or her certificates or stopping a foreclosure on his or her property.

So the question is how do you make money on tax sale certificates? Well, you start by either going to tax sale certificate sales, bidding on tax sale certificates, or buying existing certificates from a tax sale certificate dealer. You're either going to get the percentage that the person who bid on the certificate bid on it or start foreclosure on the property. At that point, you will get all your money back plus the percentage of the interest or you'll get the property. It's a "no lose" situation and it's guaranteed by the government. So after you start your investing in tax sale certificates, you must decide if you're going to make money from the interest or by foreclosing or both. You might decide just to be a tax sale certificate dealer by buying and selling tax sale certificates for a profit.

The longer you keep the certificate, the more its worth. In addition to the interest you're getting, you can put a premium on the certificate. The closer it is to foreclosure, the more its worth. So now you're going to start purchasing tax sale certificates from towns across the US or from the tax sale certificate dealers. Some states have very high percentages that they pay, like Illinois pays 36 percent in taxes and Texas has 25 percent for most properties when redeemed within six months. If the property owner redeems in one month, the effective interest rate is 300 percent.

If you buy ten tax sale certificates and you get one foreclosure out of it, you will easily make 100 percent on your investments. I have been a tax sale certificate dealer for the last fifteen years. And I can tell you that is the way to go. If you want to share your investment with other people, you can always do syndication on the venture and share your profits and loses with other people. If you want to use other people's money, you can form syndication and be the general partner of a limited partnership, that way you take all the loss responsibility but share in the profit of the investment. If you want more information on the tax sale certificates, go to dommicoinvestments.com and click on tax sale certificates or just Google tax sale certificates.

Chapter 50

Large Development Twenty Million Dollar Build Out

A GOOD FRIEND OF mine called me one day and asked me to find tenants for his huge development. He purchased a 475-acre piece of land on the Atlantic City expressway right before the Atlantic City, or Absecon Island as it's called, which is only six square miles. So adding 475 acres on was quite an accomplishment. The acreage was wetland and had to get approvals in order to make the most of its uplands. My friend, by filling in lots of the wetland with sand from the bottom of the adjacent bay, was able to get over one hundred acres of uplands approved.

We got an approval for a fashion mall for fifty thousand square feet, ten non-casino hotel/motel sites, approximately 1,200 rooms, five fast-food sites, a day-care center, twelve casino billboards, and six hundred casino parking places. The DOT (Department of Transportation) agreed to put the infrastructure in, paving roads, and putting up street lights, etc., and credit the six hundred parking places in on the property where they were already in between the expressway that we had 8,400 running feet on. The DOT was going to pay us much for each parking place each day, whether they were filled or not. The tenants for the hotel site were to be six brand-name hotels to do business when the rooms in Atlantic City were filled up on weekends.

After we put the deal together, it took about six years. The biggest thing we had to overcome was the task of getting this large area of wetland converted to fifty acres of upland; it was the largest wetland to upland approval ever in the state. The land was on the expressway and was only two minutes before Atlantic City.

While I was doing so much work in Atlantic City, I got many other opportunities at the same time. Another friend of mine had a motel that was across the street from three hundred condominiums that where built on the beach, but were never sold out.

In Atlantic City, in order to have a casino, you need five hundred rooms, 25,000 square foot of gambling area, and parking. I decided to put the three hundred condos and the 250 motel rooms across the street for sale and build a bridge across the street between the two buildings. I had an architect draw a rendering of a bridge and what the finished casino would look like. Instead of spending three hundred million dollars to build a casino, you could have put this deal together for under fifty million.

So I decided to go to Nevada and talk to some mom-and-pop casino operators to try to put this casino deal together. I landed in Reno, rented a car, and drove the whole state of Nevada, talking to many casino operators, trying to put this deal together, but had no success.

After I got back, I got a call from another friend of mine who had an option on a piece of land, about 3.5 acres, who wanted to build a casino that was to be like a mall. The casino would be operated by a casino operator, the parking lot would be rented from a parking lot company, and the restaurants would be rented by five or six restaurant chains. The whole casino was to be rented out. My friend promised to pay me one million dollars to put the deal together; that is, getting all the tenants together. My friend tried to get a loan I remember from a bank from Copenhagen, Denmark, and after I got the whole thing tenanted, he wasn't able to get a loan to build the casino.

After that, I got approached by another guy who was trying to purchase an existing casino that was closed and he wanted to buy the place and make a casino for Asian people with an Asian building, with Asian dealers, waitresses, and bartenders, strictly for Asian players, which represent a large percentage of the gamblers in Atlantic City. After he drew the renderings of the casino that he wanted to build, the deal fell apart. After that, I decided I would try anything, so I decided to put several deals together on several large restaurants.

Chapter 51

Making Large Parcels of Land into Millions of Dollars

ANOTHER FRIEND OF MINE once found a piece of land that was one thousand acres and was landlocked. In front of this landlocked property was a seven-acre piece of land that gives access to an interstate exit. My friend purchased the one thousand acres of land for $500 an acre and then purchased the seven acres for $250,000, putting a price of $750,000 for the whole piece of land. The property was zoned for one-acre lots; my friend was able to get seven hundred one-acre lots out of this property, which he sold to a developer for $10,000 a lot.

It is possible to make millions of dollars on property subdivisions; you just have to look for them. Finding large pieces of land and subdividing them into parcels whether they are residential, commercial, or industrial is as profitable as finding the right use for the right area. There is also a lot of money in changing uses from what they are to a higher and better use, which is worth a lot more money.

Gathering land when you find out that someone is putting in a new highway where there wasn't one before can be very beneficial in making large deals like this. Its takes a lot of guts to invest in these kinds of deals, but remember, you can always do that limited partnership with you as general partner, where you can share the risk with many other investors and will still seal the deal out if it fails to get 50 percent instead of 100 percent of what you expected out of it. You have to be able to change your plan after you get into it, an alternate plan if you will. You can change your idea with land easily when whatever you are trying to do with it doesn't work for one reason or another. Land has many uses unlike anything else; you just have to have imagination.

Chapter 52

The Great Approval Process

I HAVE A FRIEND of mine who was in the automotive industry who used to purchase options on land contingent upon getting it approved or development. In my earlier days, I was a commercial/industrial real estate broker. My friend always hired me to do his deals for him. I would go in and get the deal in contract, contingent upon getting whatever approvals were needed to get the deal done and get the deal approved, then sell it to a developer. We would purchase the land and hire an architect and an engineer to get the approval for us and then we would sell the deal to a developer who would build it and sell it to an investor or a group of investors who would rent it out after it was built or sell it to a chain, such as Circuit City, and whatever other chain wanted to go into the deal with them.

We did several shopping centers, an industrial park, and a professional campus before the market turned bad, as it does about every seven years or so. If you check back over the last fifty or so years, you'll find out that every seven years, we have some kind of recession. The biggest deal we did was a hundred-acre waterfront property next to an oil refinery We went in and got it all approved for detached and semidetached homes, condos, a large shopping center, a large fashion mall, five hundred boat slips for a boat mall to sell boats of many brands, a commercial park, and a huge office complex. A ferry boat would take you to the city across the waterway, so you could live in the complex and take a ferry boat and go to work every day without taking your car and paying to park it in the city.

We were selling the approved complex to an Asian group. I remember the day they came in by helicopter and landed right in the middle of the site to look around. After that, we did a forty-acre mall, built it out, and sold it to a developer. There is a lot of money to be made in getting land approved and selling it to investors or users. You can again do it yourself with syndication or do it yourself without a group. The main thing is to get in agreements contingent upon getting your approvals. Once you get in agreements, as long as you do everything it says on that agreement, you have complete control over that large piece of real estate. And you really never have to purchase the property yourself, you can do an assignment agreement and assign the agreements to someone else and have them go to settlement.

When you make the agreements of sale, make sure it says Robert Domico, or assignee, or nominee, or New Jersey Corporation to be formed, hereafter known as buyer. Then you can syndicate, you can assign, you can flip the deal, or whatever comes down the pike. Remember, you can always use other people's credibility and other people's money to do a deal; that way, you will never lose anything. I hope you were able to get a lot of ideas out of my book.

Good luck!

www.ingramcontent.com/pod-product-compliance
Lightning Source LLC
LaVergne TN
LVHW011928070526
838202LV00054B/4540